Canadian Biography Series

BIG BEAR
(MISTAHIMUSQUA)

E98.C8 B546 1996
0134107631282
Miller, J. R. (James Rodger), 1943-
Big Bear (Mistahimusqua) /
c1996.

Big Bear as sketched by C.W. Jeffreys.

Big Bear

(MISTAHIMUSQUA)

J.R. Miller

ECW PRESS

Copyright © ECW PRESS, 1996

All rights reserved. No part of this publication may be reproduced, stored in a retrieval system, or transmitted in any form by any process — electronic, mechanical, photocopying, recording, or otherwise — without the prior written permission of the copyright owners and ECW PRESS.

CANADIAN CATALOGUING IN PUBLICATION DATA

Miller, J.R. (James Rodger), 1943–
Big Bear (Mistahimusqua)
Includes bibliographical references.
ISBN 1-55022-272-4

1. Big Bear, 1825–1888. 2 Cree Indians – History.
3. Cree Indians – Biography. 4. Indians of North America – Prairie Provinces – Biography. 1. Title.

E99.C88B5 1996 971.2004973 C95-932850-5

This book has been published with the assistance of the Ministry of Culture, Tourism and Recreation of the Province of Ontario, through funds provided by the Ontario Publishing Centre, and with the assistance of grants from the Department of Communications, The Canada Council, the Ontario Arts Council, and the Government of Canada through the Canadian Studies and Special Projects Directorate of the Department of the Secretary of State of Canada.

Design and imaging by ECW Type & Art, Oakville, Ontario.
Printed by Imprimerie Gagné, Louiseville, Quebec.

Distributed by General Distribution Services,
30 Lesmill Road, Don Mills, Ontario M3B 2T6.
(416) 445-3333, (800) 387-0172 (Canada), FAX (416) 445-5967.

Distributed to the trade in the United States exclusively
by InBook, 140 Commerce Street, P.O. Box 120261,
East Haven, Connecticut, U.S.A. 06512.
Customer service: (800) 243-0138, FAX (800) 334-3892.

Distributed in the United Kingdom by Cardiff Academic Press,
St. Fagan's Road, Fairwater, Cardiff, Wales CF5 3AE.
(01222) 560333, FAX (01222) 554909.

Published by ECW PRESS,
2120 Queen Street East, Suite 200
Toronto, Ontario M4E 1E2.

ACKNOWLEDGEMENTS

Archivists and librarians at the National Archives of Canada, Saskatchewan Archives Board, and Glenbow Archives gave advice on sources and illustrations in their usual, efficient manner. Dr. Robert S. Allen, an acknowledged authority on Native history, generously assisted with information on his own published work on Big Bear and research notes on the North West Mounted Police that he had made. My colleague Dr. Bill Waiser answered innumerable questions and provided copies of several key sources. I am grateful to all these people.

The Office of Research Services of the University of Saskatchewan, directed by Dr. Michael Owen, provided assistance from the Publications Fund to procure copies of some of the archival photographs and to prepare the map used in this book. The map was skilfully drawn by Keith Bigelow, cartographic technician, Department of Geography, University of Saskatchewan.

Dallas Harrison provided expert and efficient copyediting that improved the prose.

Finally and most importantly, I am, as usual, indebted to my wife, Mary, who not only considered queries and offered suggestions but also located and copied several primary sources for me.

This brief study of a key figure in both Cree and Canadian history is dedicated to the Plains peoples.

PHOTOGRAPHS: Cover photo, National Archives of Canada, C 1873; frontispiece illustration, sketch by C.W. Jefferys, National Archives of Canada, C 69930; illustration 1, map by Keith Bigelow, University of Saskatchewan; illustration 2, National Archives of Canada, PA 31615, illustration 3, National Archives of Canada, C 5181; illustration 4, National Archives of Canada, C 33472; illustration 5, National Archives of Canada, PA 118768; illustration 6, Royal Ontario Museum 913.13.60, is used by permission of Royal Ontario Museum; illustration 7, sketch by Lt. Back, RN , 8 Feb. 1820, National Archives of Canada, C 33615; illustration 8, watercolour by A.J. Miller, 1867, National Archives of Canada, C 403; illustration 9, *Canadian Illustrated News*, 9 Sept. 1871, National Archives of Canada, C 56481; illustration 10, A.C. McIntyre, after a sketch by M. Bastien in *Canadian Illustrated News*, 16 Dec. 1876, National Archives of Canada, C 64741; illustration 11, National Archives of Canada, C 70758; illustration 12, National Archives of Canada, C 18892; illustration 13, G.M. Dawson, 6 June 1883, National Archives of Canada, PA 50749; illustration 14, G.M. Dawson, 6 June 1883, National Archives of Canada, PA 50746; illustration 15, *Illustrated War News*, 20 June 1885, is used by permission of Glenbow Archives, NA 1353-21; illustration 16, Arthur DePatie, is used by permission of Glenbow Archives, NA 4154-3; illustration 17, T.B. Strange, is used by permission of Glenbow Archives, NA 1817-5; illustration 18, *Canadian Pictorial and Illustrated War News*, 2 July 1885, is used by permission of Glenbow Archives, NA 1480-38; illustration 19, *Illustrated War News*, is used by permission of Glenbow Archives, NA 1353-16; illustration 20, Fred A. Russell and Kalamazoo Public Library, Kalamazoo, MI, is used by permission of Glenbow Archives, NA 635-3; illustration 21 is used by permission of Glenbow Archives, NA 119-1; illustration 22, C.B. Buell, is used by permission of Glenbow Archives, NA 3205-11; illustration 23, William Pearce, is used by permission of Glenbow Archives, NA 20-2; illustration 24, Public Archives of Manitoba, is used by permission of Glenbow Archives, NA 1315-18; and illustration 25, Hall and Lowe and Public Archives of Manitoba, is used by permission of Glenbow Archives, NA 1315-17.

TABLE OF CONTENTS

ACKNOWLEDGEMENTS 5
LIST OF ILLUSTRATIONS 8

Big Bear (Mistahimusqua) 11

CHRONOLOGY 128
WORKS CONSULTED 131

LIST OF ILLUSTRATIONS

	Big Bear in jail, 1885	cover
	Big Bear as sketched by C.W. Jeffreys	*frontispiece*
1.	Big Bear's World	9
2.	Buffalo	20
3.	Cree camp near Vermilion, Alberta, 1871	29
4.	Cree family with horse and travois	30
5.	Big Bear trading at Fort Pitt, c. 1884	38
6.	Mistahimusqua, armed	45
7.	Buffalo pound	52
8.	Buffalo jump	54
9.	Negotiations at Stone Fort (Winnipeg), 1871	67
10.	Treaty Six talks at Fort Carlton, 1876	70
11.	Treaty medal	74
12.	Blackfoot chief wearing medal and triennial suit	76
13.	Big Bear's camp near Maple Creek, 1883	88
14.	Watering horses at Big Bear's camp, 1883	89
15.	Theresa Gowanlock, prisoner of Wandering Spirit, 1885	104
16.	Pursuit of Big Bear, 1885	109
17.	General Strange's sketch of Frenchman's Butte	111
18.	Big Bear's surrender	113
19.	Big Bear captured by Strange	114
20.	Horse Child, Big Bear's youngest son, 1885	116
21.	W.B. Cameron, pro-Big Bear witness, and Horse Child, 1885	117
22.	Horse Child, Big Bear, and Poundmaker with police and priests, 1885	119
23.	On steps of Stony Mountain Penitentiary, 1886	121
24.	Big Bear and Poundmaker in prison, 1886	123
25.	Big Bear in prison, 1886	125

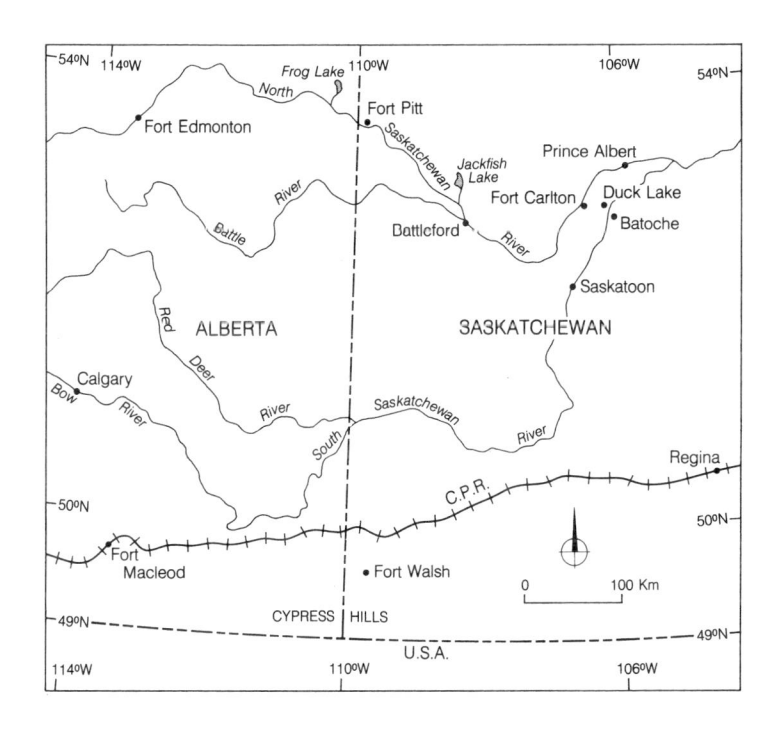

FIGURE I

Big Bear's world.

Big Bear

(MISTAHIMUSQUA)

AT JACKFISH LAKE

Some fifty kilometres north of the junction of the Battle and the North Saskatchewan Rivers, Jackfish Lake sparkles as the warm sun returns in the spring. Settled into the rolling, lightly wooded country that is typical of the Prairie parkland region, it has long served as a rich source of fish, wood, and water for a succession of human populations, both Aboriginal and non-Native. The parkland appeals in the twentieth century to urban populations seeking outdoor recreation, occasionally as in the case of fishing and hunting parties, and seasonally in the case of the middle-class families from Saskatoon and other places who relocate in the warm weather to cottages on Jackfish Lake. For those who cannot afford or do not favour cottage life, camping is available for trailers, mobile homes, and tents in Battleford Provincial Park, which touches one side of the lake. When campers, hunters, or cottagers make their way to Jackfish Lake, they quickly encounter several Native populations, some Métis and some Cree, on reserves and in settlements in the region. Ironically, these groups are descendants of Aboriginal communities that, two centuries ago and more, treated Jackfish Lake in a way that is the mirror image of that of the non-Natives seeking recreation there today. For groups of Cree, Saulteaux, and even some

Assiniboine and Dakota, the parkland region served as a home base, particularly during the harsh winter months when its wood and its shelter in the lee of hills and wooded slopes made it a haven, from which they ranged out at other times to hunt for food, to bargain with the strangers at their distant trading forts, and, all too often, to engage in raids and warfare against other Aboriginal groups.

Into this setting the man those strangers would call Big Bear was born in 1825. Son of Black Powder, chief of a small band, and a woman whose name has not survived, to his own people he was known as Mistahimusqua. Black Powder was an Ojibwa (or Saulteaux), his wife either a Cree or an Ojibwa, and the band that he led a mixture of Cree and Ojibwa inhabiting a region dominated by Cree bands. Black Powder, or Mukatai in the language of his own people, was known for his audacity in making war, particularly against a traditional foe such as the Blackfoot, a confederacy of nations that lived far to the southwest. Mukatai was known to European traders as well, such as the Hudson's Bay employees at Carlton House on the North Saskatchewan.

In the Plains society into which Big Bear was born, it was not considered strange that his father led a mixed community of Cree and Ojibwa. Such a motley arrangement was by no means unusual in the 1820s, no more than the ethnically mixed background of young Big Bear himself. The Cree, originally a woodlands people from the Canadian Shield country southwest of James Bay, had moved south and west from the early 1700s onward in response to economic opportunities that arose in the fur trade. Pursuing trade opportunities over many decades, they had migrated in particular along the course of the Saskatchewan River into the heart of the prairie west.

As the Cree penetrated the plains, they came into contact, and sometimes into collision, with other groups. They often mixed in with Ojibwa, like themselves originally a woodlands hunting-and-gathering people who had moved west for economic reasons. In the west, the Ojibwa were often referred to as Saulteaux.

(Increasing the possibility of misunderstanding, they were usually labelled Chippewa in the United States.) The Cree and Ojibwa also cooperated for trade purposes with the Assiniboine, a people of Siouan linguistic stock, who had entered the region from the south. The shifting commercial and military ties of Cree, Ojibwa, and Assiniboine were often necessary for defence against the large and well-organized nations of the Blackfoot Confederacy in what is now southern Alberta. Big Bear's father, then, was one human link in a vast economic and military chain that joined a variety of Indigenous peoples, an extensive network that stretched from the foothills of the Rocky Mountains to the shores of James Bay and Hudson Bay, and even to the non-Native merchants and bankers of London across the ocean.

For Big Bear, of course, growing up in Black Powder's lodge, such weighty considerations of economics and war were totally irrelevant. Rather, his early years were shaped by the patterns of family life, the social organization of Plains peoples, and the worldview of Aboriginal peoples generally. Mistahimusqua matured and learned his people's ways in Black Powder's extended family, the centre of his early universe. Like other boys, he found the role of a male child a privileged and enjoyable one. Among both Plains Cree and Saulteaux, the days of childhood were a time of apparently endless recreation and freedom. Big Bear was indulged by adults, and few requirements were placed upon him in the early years. So he and his friends grew up with their basic needs for food, clothing, and shelter provided for by their parents as generously as the sometimes precarious hunting, fishing, and trading economy would allow.

There were few formal rules of behaviour that bound Big Bear and his mates. In the encampment on the shores of Jackfish Lake, as elsewhere in Plains society, youngsters were permitted and even expected to while away their days in freedom. This was merely a special form of the respect for liberty typical of Plains society in general, a way of life in which deliberate interference with the freedom of action of another individual was considered inappropriate. Rather, the social ethics of Plains peoples relied on persuasion, bonds of family and kin obligations, and the use of ridicule to promote desired conduct and discourage antisocial behaviour. To the unfamiliar eye of an outsider, the life that Big Bear and other children lived in communities such as the one that Black Powder led in the 1820s and 1830s was a paradise of freedom, recreation, and enjoyment.

As Big Bear gradually learned, however, life for a Native child, even the son of a chief, was more complex than it first appeared. For one thing, a lack of rules did not mean an absence of limitations. Even Black Powder's son soon came to realize that if his and his mates' actions violated what their community expected, they would be treated to stern disapproval from parents and other adults. On one occasion, when Big Bear and his friends got into a scrape, the story that an elder told that evening around the fire where children gathered to listen to tales featured a disobedient youngster who came to a bad end as a result of his unruly and selfish behaviour. Storytelling, which happened most evenings in the wintertime in particular, was one of the most important ways in which Black Powder's following, like Plains peoples in general, taught their youngsters how to behave. If Big Bear did something unkind or selfish during the day, he would, without ever hearing his name mentioned in the story, be informed implicitly during storytelling time in the evening that such conduct was not acceptable.

When the elders were not indirectly chastising the youngsters of the band by stories, they were teaching them their people's religious beliefs, history, and intimate knowledge of the natural world by the same means. Other stories would tell about how the Creator made the world, gave the various animals their names and defining characteristics, and taught human beings, such as the Cree, how to behave in his world. The great deeds of their ancestors, especially in warfare against the Blackfoot Confederacy, would be recounted in great detail to Big Bear and the other round-eyed children, who hung on every word as the old one's voice spun the tale and the firelight flickered. Stories from the respected adults of the community was the most important way in which Plains children were educated. It was through tales, legends, and examples from adults that the young Big Bear learned who he was, what his people had done, and what was expected of them and himself.

Also important to his education were the games and other recreational activities that he and his friends were encouraged to take up and perfect. Men in the band would make a bow and some arrows for the boys, thereby stimulating them to play games that taught them skills of hunting and fighting. Even activities that disrupted the band, such as "raids" by marauding boys who stole fish that had been set out to dry over a fire or "thefts" perpetrated by youngsters who pounced on food delights, were treated with amused forbearance. Tolerant adults knew that the thieving rapscallions were learning skills that would stand them in good stead in later raids on an enemy's camp. The first time that Big Bear brought home some small game he had killed with an arrow, Black Powder and the other adults made a great fuss over his exploit. The grownups organized a special feast in which the prize brought in by the chief's son was ceremonially served in tiny portions to everyone in the lodge, and the youthful mighty hunter was praised lavishly for his skill. These community practices reinforced the love of hunting in Big Bear and the other youngsters.

Girls, too, had their behaviour quietly shaped by the women of the community. Their games often revolved around maternal skills, such as child care (which could be absorbed in part from playing with dolls), and domestic activities, such as cleaning and preparing food. For the girls, the parallel to the fuss made over their brothers' first kill of game was the celebration over berries gathered and prepared for a meal or some other "first food" occurrence. Although the boys and girls in Black Powder's camp probably did not realize it until much later (when they fostered the same kinds of behaviour in their own children), their apparently aimless and pleasurable way of life was in fact part of their education in Plains society. Lacking classrooms, Big Bear and the other children had elders who told gripping stories; in the absence of formal job-related training, they learned to hunt, raid, and fight through games approved and encouraged by the adults of the community.

All the children learned their people's understanding of the deity and the world around them in the same way. Adults never missed a chance to explain why a particular animal had the physical characteristics it did. The contributions and expectations of the Creator were also spelled out by means of stories and examples. By these means, Big Bear grew up knowing that he was kin to everything in nature around him. He and everyone else in the band were related to the tree people, the fish people, and the animal people because those things had been put on the earth by the Creator and had, as they did themselves, spirits. The souls or spirits of all the other parts of creation had to be shown respect and treated in the proper way in order not to upset them and cause harm to the humans. So, for example, stories that Big Bear heard in the evenings around the fire explained that people did not throw fish or animal bones into the flames because such disrespectful treatment would offend the spirits of the fish or the beaver or buffalo. And affronted spirits of the fish would take their revenge on the human animals who had insulted them and their kinfolk by warning other fish to avoid the humans' nets or spears, with the result that the fish would not be caught and the humans would suffer for their disrespectful behaviour toward their kin.

A more positive feature of these views was the teaching that offerings should be made to the Creator and sometimes to the animals or even natural features such as dangerous waterfalls. Humans should always thank the Creator for a new day and ask his blessing on their activities, such as hunting or going to war or discussing peace with old enemies. In these and other ways, Big Bear and the young people with whom he grew up learned their place in the world and their obligations to the Creator and all other forms of life, with whom they shared the land. Their "religious" education — for this is what the stories and rituals were — taught them that Cree and Ojibwa were part of an intricate web of life that included not just humans and animals and fish but also the physical features of their world. They knew that they were involved in a real and continuous way with everything else in their world.

THE PLAINS HUNTING LIFE

While they were growing up, Big Bear and the other children only gradually came to learn of the wider human community of which the Plains Indians were a part. Beyond the shores of Jackfish Lake, Black Powder's band was involved in complex networks of economic and military relations with other Native communities and with strangers from across the ocean. The most important factor in the pattern of relations that had developed by the time Big Bear was born in 1825 was the trade in furs that had been going on with Europeans for a century and a half. Englishmen representing the Hudson's Bay Company had been purchasing furs at posts at the mouths of rivers that drained into James Bay and Hudson Bay since the 1670s, but they had been coming into the interior of the region from the 1770s onward. And starting in the 1790s, Scottish and French-Canadian traders from Montreal had begun to invade the northwest after long trips by canoe. In the twenty or thirty years before Big Bear was born, the competition between these Montreal traders, often known as the Northwest Company or Nor'westers, and the Hudson's Bay Company personnel had been intense and often destructive to Native peoples. The struggle for control of the fur trade had led to the widespread use of violence and the abuse of alcohol to gain and hold Cree, Blackfoot, Chipewyan, and other Native traders, with a resulting serious loss for the Indigenous peoples. This destructive/competitive phase of the fur trade had come to an end in 1821, when the Bay absorbed the Northwest Company.

By the time Big Bear was born, all the Native peoples of the western interior had become involved directly or indirectly in the commerce in furs. For some, such as the Cree and Ojibwa, who had begun moving from the woodlands southwest to the prairies and parklands in the early 1700s, their very presence in the region was a direct result of the Europeans' trade in furs. The Cree and Assiniboine had developed the role of an intermediary between some of the more distant Indian nations and the Europeans, making a profit on the trade in both directions. The price of iron goods obtained from an Englishman or a Canadian they would mark up when selling them in turn to a Chipewyan; they would also pay the Native supplier of a pelt much less than they would get for it at a fur trader's post. The Europeans' fur trade exerted a strong influence on the economic activities of the peoples in the western interior, including groups such as Black Powder's following.

The fur trade was an important factor in the seasonal behaviour of Big Bear's community. Furs acquired either by hunting or from other Natives through trade or war would be exchanged at a Hudson's Bay Company post such as Fort Carlton on the North Saskatchewan River, about one hundred kilometres overland and much farther by river to the southeast from Jackfish Lake. The major trade alternative in the early days was Edmonton House far up the North Saskatchewan to the west, but it was too close to territory controlled by enemies of the Cree and Ojibwa to be very attractive. Even Black Powder, who was somewhat rash about getting involved in conflict, would not go as far as Fort Edmonton to trade. A safer and much closer substitute was Fort Pitt, which the Bay set up on the North Saskatchewan about one hundred kilometres to the west in 1834, more to gather in food provisions than to trade in furs. As events turned out, Black Powder and later Big Bear kept their trading activities focused for many decades on the older post at Fort Carlton, ranging back and forth between it and Jackfish Lake in warmer times of the year. Also important to their seasonal movements were the herds of buffalo on the plains to the south and west of their home territory. They would often set out in pursuit of these magnificent animals, which ranged the prairies and up into the parklands in herds that sometimes numbered in the tens of thousands. From the buffalo, they got not just shaggy pelts to trade but also food, clothing, tent skins, and even fuel from the manure. The pursuit of the buffalo and the trade opportunities of Fort Carlton in particular were what periodically drew them away (except in winter) from their comfortable home base by Jackfish Lake.

As an adolescent, Big Bear experienced firsthand one of the negative results of mixing with the Europeans. In addition to providing new and expanded economic opportunities, the fur trade brought to the region less desirable effects: epidemics, hardship, and intensified warfare. From time to time, outbreaks of disease were brought to the plains unknowingly by Englishmen or, later, Americans. Some of these diseases, such as smallpox, were terribly deadly for Aboriginal groups exposed to them because they had not built up resistance to the diseases, as Europeans and Americans had through repeated if sporadic exposure to them. Even ailments that did not cause serious harm to the Europeans, such as measles, were often fatal for Plains and other Aboriginal peoples because of this lack of acquired immunity. The fur trade, which brought outsiders and their goods into the western region and spread them far and wide, proved to be a mechanism for transmitting the microbes, bacteria, and viruses of disease as well. When Big Bear was still a boy, during the 1837–38 season, one such outbreak of smallpox proved devastating to most of the Plains peoples. In his case, his face remained pitted with the disease's pockmarks long after he recovered, disfiguring him for the rest of his life and making him self-conscious about his less than impressive appearance. For a number of the Plains peoples, this epidemic proved far more serious. Some groups, such as the Assiniboine and Mandan, lost so many of their people to the Europeans' disease that they were permanently weakened and their role in the fur trade forever reduced.

A second negative consequence of the coming of the English or Canadian fur trader, one that would affect Big Bear later in life, was the increased pressure on the food resources of the

FIGURE 2

Buffalo.

western region, a pressure that would eventually cause hardship, hunger, and even starvation for many people. In a very real sense, the Europeans' fur trade encouraged the development of relationships and forces that enormously increased the strain on all kinds of resources in the western plains and woodlands. It was not that Native peoples had not indulged in trade and harvested the food and mineral resources of the region long before the Bay men and Montreal-based voyageurs came on the scene. The well-established trade routes and links in operation when these traders turned up were the foundation of the broader, more market-oriented trade that developed after 1670. Groups such as the Cree and Assiniboine, who responded to the trade opportunities by moving west and becoming trading intermediaries, were merely reacting to another in a succession of economic factors, in this case the coming of the European and Canadian. However, this time the change had a significant qualitative difference, one that would weigh heavily on western resources.

The Europeans who traded with Black Powder and other leaders at posts such as Fort Carlton created a heavy demand for animal skins and foodstuffs, a need that far exceeded anything known before. At first, it was merely the novelty of a new source of demand — the Bay men at their posts at the mouths of rivers — that stimulated Native peoples to harvest more animals for their furs and food. Then it was the intense competition between Nor'westers and Bay traders that drove up prices and increased the desirability of supplying furs. The same competition pushed the fur traders farther north and west into the Athabasca country, as the vast territory drained by rivers flowing to the Arctic Ocean was known to the Europeans. Even after the competition was removed in 1821 by amalgamation of the two fur-trading companies, the expansion of trading activity into the far northern country maintained the demand on prairie food sources in particular. Increasingly, trading forts in the river valleys of the south were designed not so much to gather in the furs themselves as to serve as assembly points for vast quantities of food. That was why Fort Pitt was founded on the North Saskatchewan in 1834; it was also the major role for Fort Carlton, the other post to which Black Powder, Big Bear, and the others usually went to trade.

The demand for food increased the pressure on the Plains Indians' major food source. Buffalo meat was the principal ingredient in the most important food on which voyageurs and traders relied. Pemmican, as it was known, was made by Indian and Métis hunters and their families from dried buffalo meat, fat, and berries all pounded into a dense, protein-rich mass and sewn into large sacks made from buffalo stomachs. Some of these containers of pemmican could weigh as much as forty kilograms, and a pemmican-producing post such as Qu'Appelle in the southern plains might gather in hundreds of such bundles for forwarding to the north.

As a chief, Big Bear would come to understand that this demand for pemmican meant heavy consumption of buffalo meat by both non-Native and Native people involved in the fur trade. From the 1830s onward, while he was a youngster growing into manhood, the pressure on the buffalo resource was increased yet again by a new market to the south, created by American traders. The demand was partly for meat and pemmican, but more particularly for hides. Buffalo skins were useful not only for clothing but also for industrial purposes. The strength and resilience of the leather made from buffalo skin made it suitable to be fashioned into the belts used to drive machinery in the growing factories of the northern American states. By the 1840s, when American traders were buying buffalo hides from Native peoples in centres such as Pembina, south of the small settlement of Red River, the trade was causing significant problems for Aboriginal communities.

Increased pressure on the buffalo resource was a major cause of warfare between a number of different groups. Again, it was not that these kinds of forces created enmities where they had not existed before; on the contrary, there had been significant warfare on the plains long before Bay men or American hide traders turned up. Usually, Aboriginal warfare had originated in a desire for revenge or in horse-stealing, both of which were important ways for young men to establish their worth in their own society. However, increasing demand on the resources of the prairies in the nineteenth century would make the conflicts much more severe, replacing motives such as exacting revenge and enhancing reputation with the strong motive of economic need.

The patterns of rivalry and warfare with which Big Bear would have to deal in adult years as a leader of his community were largely the result of geography and trading relationships. Within the memory of a chief such as Black Powder, the Cree had worked within an informal alliance with the Blackfoot that supplied the Cree with the horses they needed to hunt buffalo and fight, and the Blackfoot with indirect access to European goods such as firearms and knives. For the Cree, such an arrangement was vital in gaining the strength that enabled them to establish themselves firmly in the northern plains and parklands. However, the Cree-Blackfoot relationship fell apart after 1810 because the Blackfoot obtained direct contact with European traders, who penetrated farther into the interior, and could obtain the desired trade goods themselves without paying markups imposed by the Cree. Now the Cree found themselves working, for both trade and military purposes, with the more southerly Mandan-Hidatsa nations of present-day United States, and they were frequently embroiled in raids against, and skirmishes with, the Blackfoot. Indeed, one of the attractions of the Jackfish Lake area to Black Powder was that it was beyond the limit of Blackfoot raiding parties. The alignments that existed from about 1810 until the middle of the century would also be loosened and destroyed by new forces. One major influence was the devastating smallpox epidemic of 1837-38, which killed so many Mandan-Hidatsa that alliance with them was no longer much of an asset for the Cree. More important, however, was the increasing competition for buffalo.

In fact, "the buffalo wars," as John Milloy terms them, dominated the plains in the period when the young Mistahimusqua was establishing his reputation and emerging as a chief. Between 1850 and 1870, there was regular, bitter conflict between different pairings of Native peoples as they pursued the dwindling herds in a time of rising demand for the products of the buffalo. One of the forerunners of this phase of prairie warfare had been the increasingly frequent clashes between the Dakota peoples south of the international boundary and the mixed-blood peoples of Red River, both the French-speaking Roman Catholics who called themselves the Métis, and the English-speaking Protestants who were known as the country born. Year by year, the huge Métis brigades would make their way out onto the plains in search of the buffalo, and steadily they were drawn farther into Dakota lands in pursuit of the animals. The Métis invasion of Siouan lands led to some major battles that formed part of the heroic history of the mixed-blood peoples of Red River. However, over time the same forces brought the Métis and others, such as the Cree and Assiniboine, into conflict with the Blackfoot far to the southwest. Throughout the middle decades of the nineteenth century, the southern plains were the site of fiercely fought battles, at the centre of which was increasingly sharp competition for a slowly diminishing food supply that was simultaneously experiencing increased demand. So significant was the problem becoming that some Cree and Saulteaux communities in the Red River and Assiniboine River valleys began to experiment with growing crops as an additional means of providing themselves with food. Groups who had long watched with interest the antics of Bay men who grew vegetables in post gardens to stretch and enrich their meagre diets now decided that copying the newcomers might make economic sense, because more and more people seemed to be hunting the buffalo.

In the time in which Big Bear grew up, the plains were both a rich and exciting and a dangerous and turbulent place to be. He experienced life in a Cree-Ojibwa community at the height of the Plains culture, founded on the three pillars of buffalo, horse, and rifle. Eventually, he was able to participate in the buffalo hunts and trips to fur-trading posts such as Fort Carlton with the other adult members of the group. At the same time, however, he found himself drawn into the increasing tensions of heightened warfare that seemed always to brood over the plains and parklands. At the centre of the looming crisis in prairie life were the excessive demands being placed on the most important thing in Plains culture, the buffalo. So Big Bear grew into adulthood in an era when buffalo hunting, trading, and raiding were the defining activities of his people. If groups such as Black Powder's people — located as they were in a relatively food-rich region and camped for long periods beside a lake well endowed with the species that gave it its name — saw no reason as yet to experiment with new ways of maintaining themselves, some other groups showed by their spontaneous interest in turnips and potatoes that they recognized the looming problem.

BECOMING A RESPECTED ADULT

Big Bear, of course, showed little or no awareness of these future challenges when he was growing up. Like other Cree and Plains youths, he was shaped by the informal educational system of adult example and storytelling while still a carefree youngster. Then, as an adolescent, he found himself increasingly involved in the raiding and small-scale warfare for which his earlier games had prepared him. As the son of a chief, he was the object of particular attention by the adult members of the community, for the expectation was that he would eventually succeed his father as chief unless he showed by some serious failings that he was not suited to the demanding role of chief of an Aboriginal community. Throughout his teens and well into his twenties, Big Bear showed that he had the skills of hunting and leadership essential to successful chieftainship. Although he was short and stocky, he demonstrated in a number of horse-stealing raids on enemy Blackfoot that he had courage and guile enough to succeed. Not even self-consciousness about a pockmarked face affected his personality in any adverse way. He was a young man of good spirits, with a lively sense of humour, often at his own expense and sometimes referring to his facial features. In many ways, he developed in a manner that befitted a typical future chief of a Plains people.

One thing that did distinguish the young Big Bear — and this, too, would stay with him his entire life — was heavy involvement in Plains religion. He developed a reputation for possessing "strong medicine," as his people described it. Possession of great spiritual powers was important to Aboriginal peoples. In their world, it was essential to keep the forces of nature in balance, especially by staying in favour with the various spirits that populated creation. Knowledge of how to please the spirit of the buffalo was essential to enjoying successful hunts; knowing how to avoid offending the spirit of the rapids in a river might ward off fatal misadventure. A woman or man who had well-developed spiritual understanding and powers could provide leadership to the community in this important area of keeping the forces of the cosmos in harmony. Such a person was referred to, with awe, as possessing strong medicine.

In the area of spiritual beliefs and practices, Mistahimusqua was notable throughout his life for his refusal to have anything to do with the new religion. Christianity, the belief system that newcomers were bringing into the country from the 1820s onward, never appealed to him. In part, his lack of interest in Christianity resulted from the fact that missionaries did not reach the part of the Saskatchewan country in which he grew up while he was still young. More likely, though, his immunity to the religion of the newcomers stemmed from his strong attachment to the traditional spiritual beliefs of his people as taught by Black Powder and other adults in the community. Big Bear showed an intense interest in Aboriginal rituals from a relatively early age. Perhaps the fact that his father was Ojibwa had something to do with his spiritual inclination: the Ojibwa enjoyed a reputation among other Plains peoples as possessing strong medicine. Big Bear became renowned as a spiritual leader to such an extent that more than a century after his death, Native elders in Saskatchewan were still reluctant to talk about him to outsiders.

Part of the reason that the Ojibwa had a reputation as a powerfully spiritual people was that their males went on what was known as the vision quest during early adolescence. This rite of passage into young adulthood involved leaving the community and going into the wilderness where, after many days of fasting and praying, the individual might receive a sign from the spirit world — from the Creator perhaps — of what one's nature and destiny were to be. The vision quest among the Ojibwa and many other Aboriginal groups was an important part of the young person's religious formation. Whether or not the young Big Bear sought such an experience in the usual Ojibwa manner is not known, but, as Hugh Dempsey explains in *Big Bear: The End of Freedom*, he did have an important vision in his early teen years. Soon after the smallpox epidemic of 1837–38, he had a vision in which the coming of white people to the lands of the Cree and Saulteaux — with the resulting loss of land and serious hardship for the original inhabitants — figured prominently. Another vision shaped the future in a more personal and positive fashion. In this revelation, Mistahimusqua was offered the opportunity to secure a large herd of horses in a cave by a spirit promising him that he would always have lots of horses. During this vision, he failed to obtain the horses because he flinched when one of the ghostly stallions reared up and seemed about to strike. Big Bear interpreted this episode as an indication that he should not keep large numbers of horses, with the result that he always gave away most of the steeds he and his fellow raiders stole from Blackfoot encampments or took from slain enemies.

However, the most important religious experience that the young Big Bear had concerned another animal. One of his visions featured the spirit of a bear, an animal greatly respected and feared in both Cree and Ojibwa societies. The bear's significance for these Aboriginal peoples came in part from its power and speed. They were also inclined to see it as an animal closely related to them because of its resemblance to humans when it reared up on its hind legs to get a better view of something. After receiving his vision of a bear, Mistahimusqua carried a bear's claw in his medicine bundle, the sack of items that had symbolic importance for individuals, often registering important visions and associating them with figures in the nonhuman world. His medicine bundle was always greatly revered by his community, and its reputation for potency enhanced his status as a man with great powers that could help to protect both him and the group from harm. People viewed Big Bear as a man possessing that all-important ability to mediate between them and the natural world about them. A reputation for having powerful medicine was just one of the many strengths that Big Bear acquired during his passage through adolescence into young manhood.

For the future chief, these years passed in a busy sequence of communal and personal events. Throughout the warmer months of the year, Black Powder's people would make their way out from the base at Jackfish Lake to trade and hunt. When they had furs to trade, their usual destination was the Hudson's Bay Company post at Fort Carlton on the North Saskatchewan, where they could obtain foodstuffs, iron products, ammunition, and, in particular, cloth. At other times, they travelled in search of migrating buffalo herds from which to get food and hides. On these occasions, the band would camp in skin tents, or tipis, near a lake or stream to guarantee having fresh water. The women of the group, in common with the women of Plains societies generally, bore heavy responsibilities. It was their job to organize the goods, look out for the children, and oversee the movement of the family, pack animals, and travois (poles dragged by a horse), which could be used to carry people or goods or both. Although these expeditions were often remembered with great fondness, they involved a lot of work, especially for the women of the group.

The major responsibilities of the men in Plains society were hunting and conducting war, diplomacy, or politics. Locating and hunting the herds of buffalo were certainly major activities

FIGURE 3

Cree camp near Vermilion, Alberta, 1871.

FIGURE 4

Cree family with horse and travois.

for the men, and stampeding the shaggy animals so that they would run over a cliff and be killed could sometimes be dangerous work for them. Much more threatening, however, were the demands of warfare, both defensive and offensive. Warfare was a vital part of the men's lives, especially in the difficult years of trade wars and competition for the buffalo after 1850 or so. Particularly when out on the prairie, a party was vulnerable to attack, perhaps by marauding Blackfoot in search of horses and goods to seize as trophies of war. A sharp watch had to be kept at night, scouts sent out from the main party during the day, and vigilance constantly exercised. When the group was detected and attacked, a defensive style of warfare was employed, in which the besieged dug themselves in in a sheltered area or in pits excavated for the purpose, from which they could fire at their attackers. The object of the defensive exercise was to inflict so much damage on the opponents that they would withdraw and leave the party alone.

Much more exciting and glamorous for a young warrior such as Big Bear was the offensive military raid. Horse-stealing raids or war parties to the country of the traditional foe, usually the Blackfoot in southern Alberta, held the potential for many benefits. There was the opportunity to strike a blow against the enemy; also significant was the chance to acquire horses in these raids. Because horses were a major form of wealth and prestige in Plains society, stolen horses were greatly desired by young warriors. In the war-oriented Plains culture, military raids were also important because they created opportunities for one to demonstrate bravery and thereby win a reputation as a respected member of the community. Achieving this end did not always involve stealing horses or killing the enemy. In some cases, a young man would improve his standing by "counting coup." This could mean sneaking into the enemy's camp under cover of darkness, creeping up on the unsuspecting foe, touching one of them, and then heading back to safety without being detected. More often, though, a fighter's reputation was made in more straightforward methods of conducting war: swooping down on an enemy band, attacking them and killing some, and making off with their horses.

Also important among the motives for going to war was revenge. Black Powder's people, along with a number of Cree bands, set out in 1847 seeking to avenge the deaths of four Cree at the hands of the Blackfoot. What was intended to be an offensive campaign turned into a defensive struggle: Black Powder and the others were besieged by an invading Blackfoot party as they made their preparations near Fort Pitt. In this instance, the Blackfoot withdrew with the goods they had seized from abandoned tents after losing ten men to their northern foe. Big Bear, now twenty-two, fought alongside his father and fortunately escaped injury. Carrying out these military activities was as important a part of the Plains male's life as hunting the buffalo or trading at Bay posts for goods.

This was the sort of life that Big Bear experienced in his teens and twenties. He would continue to learn by watching his elders as they decided when to travel to trade, where and when to hunt the buffalo, and how to guard against enemy attacks. He would also, on rare occasions, have a chance to learn of the other role of chiefs and leading men, the practice of diplomacy, which was almost as important as hunting and fighting in the Plains culture of his time. Big Bear and the other men his age also spent a lot of time during the nonwinter months planning and carrying out raids against their enemies.

Big Bear was now reaching full manhood. An experienced hunter and fighter, he enjoyed the respect of his family and neighbours. Already carrying a reputation for spiritual powers, he was also held in awe for his visions and religious association with his namesake, the bear. The final way in which Big Bear established himself as a worthy member of his community was to marry sometime near the end of the 1840s. The first of what would eventually be a total of five wives was an Ojibwa woman named Sayos, who would bear him two daughters and two sons. The daughter, Nowakich, was followed by Twin Wolverine, then Bad Child or Imasees (also known by his second name, Little

Bear, Apistakoos in Cree), and Horse Child. Marriage to Sayos continued the family tendency to combine Ojibwa and Cree elements, though Black Powder's and Big Bear's way of life by now resembled that of the Plains Cree almost completely, with few relics of their woodlands-based Ojibwa heritage. Marrying Sayos, whose family had moved west and mixed with Cree groups (much as Black Powder and his people had done), effectively symbolized that amalgamation of Ojibwa or Saulteaux and Plains Cree cultures.

On a more personal level, marriage and parenthood opened a new chapter in Big Bear's already eventful life. Although he would continue to have responsibilities in hunting and fighting, henceforth he would have to be more concerned about the welfare of his immediate and growing family. This meant participation in fewer of the raids the young men continued to organize into Blackfoot country and concentration on feeding his family and raising his children properly — these would be his preoccupations.

CHIEF BIG BEAR

Throughout the 1850s and 1860s, while Big Bear focused on his duties as a family man and the chief's son, the environment in which his people lived began to change for the worse. These were years of continuing pressure on Plains peoples in general, as the demand for buffalo remained high from both the Hudson's Bay Company and American purchasers. Probably unknown to Black Powder's group, which ranged from the North Saskatchewan River down to the Red Deer River, were the beginnings of settlement in the Red River valley farther to the east. This scattering of shacks and cabins was the forerunner of a much more extensive invasion of the plains by non-Natives, an invasion that would have a profound effect on all Plains peoples, including those around Black Powder and Big Bear.

In the 1850s, though, life still seemed good for the young father and warrior. The annual cycles of hunting and trading went on, sometimes punctuated by raids by the Blackfoot. The Fort Pitt region became a hotly contested area between Cree and Blackfoot by the 1860s, as the southern group sought revenge for losses at the hands of the river Cree, as those along the North Saskatchewan were known. Occasional attempts at peacemaking occurred, as in 1862, to put an end to Cree-Blackfoot hostilities, but they did not prove successful in the long run.

The twin scourges of warfare and disease had a direct impact on Big Bear and Black Powder before too long. On one occasion in 1863, Big Bear almost got caught up in a Blackfoot attack while he was at Fort Pitt to trade. He was deeply involved in the formal speeches and exchanges of so-called gifts with the trader when a scout brought word that a large body of Blackfoot warriors was approaching. Big Bear was able to avoid any trouble by staying inside the post until the enemy force passed on. Epidemics, however, could not be avoided as easily, as the Blackfoot and the Cree along the North Saskatchewan discovered in 1864 and 1865. They suffered serious losses of life to various ailments. It was about this time that Big Bear's father died, though it is not clear whether he fell victim to disease, warfare, or simply age. Whatever the cause, his departure for the Sand Hills — as the Cree termed the afterlife — removed from his band a man who had served them well. Black Powder had a well-earned reputation for leadership in both peace and war, and his passing was greatly lamented by his family and followers.

For Big Bear, the death of his father meant another major change in his way of life. Black Powder's journey to the Sand Hills raised, of course, the question of who should succeed him as chief of the group, and it was obvious that Big Bear was the logical candidate. Among Plains societies, the office of chief was hereditary under certain conditions; if the deceased chief's son had not distinguished himself as a hunter and warrior, and if he did not have personal qualities that made people willing to deal with him, he might be barred from assuming his father's office.

In such a case, a more qualified and worthy man would emerge to carry out the functions of the leader and eventually be recognized as chief of the band.

However, no one questioned Big Bear's assuming the title that heredity made available to him. He was an experienced and proficient hunter, and he had served with distinction in a number of military campaigns over the previous twenty years. In fact, his military prowess had long since made him a member of the warrior society and the "Worthy Young Men" of the community. And Big Bear was regarded as a pleasant fellow with a good sense of humour, someone who did not take himself (or his physical appearance) too seriously. He related easily and well with other members of his community. Finally, he enjoyed a reputation as someone with strong spiritual powers, an extremely important attainment in Plains society, though not a quality absolutely necessary in a chief. Mistahimusqua's spiritual association with the mighty bear, symbolized by the bear claw in his medicine bundle, was a potent quality. His strong medicine merely enhanced his standing, making him indisputably the logical person to succeed the late and lamented Black Powder.

To the modern observer, what is less clear is why anyone would have wanted to be the chief of a traditional Plains community. Chieftainship was not an opportunity for power and wealth; rather, it was a sentence of obligation. The chief, though respected, did not derive material benefits from his office. On the contrary, he was expected to help provide for the poor and sick, to contribute more than others to communal celebrations, and to act as much the servant as the leader of his people. It was also his role to act as peacemaker between members of the group in conflict, and he was expected to play this role mainly by example and action. Big Bear experienced this burden directly on one occasion, when a drunken member of his band attacked and struck him. As soon as his daughter saw what had happened to her father, she responded by ripping the assailant's tepee and taking some of his possessions from the dwelling. When Big Bear regained consciousness, he issued instructions that his assailant's goods were to be returned to him immediately and that no one was to do anything further to punish his attacker for what he had done. Such restrained behaviour was typically required of a chief, who led by example as much as by words and deeds. Also typical was the aftermath of this attack. Big Bear's assailant tried to make amends later on, but he was rebuffed and suffered a serious loss of prestige in the eyes of the people of his community. Both Big Bear's behaviour and his attacker's fate at the hands of his neighbours underlined the importance of status, reputation, and prestige among the Plains peoples. Material goods such as horses and household effects were much less important in making a person's reputation than good conduct. The best behaviour involved service, sacrifice, forbearance, and forgiveness. Chieftainship was a form of service.

Contact with the European fur trader had caused some weakening of the traditional aspects of Plains chieftainship. The Hudson's Bay Company systematically both honoured and undermined some chiefs for its own economic purposes. As part of its adoption of Native methods of conducting trade, the company would show special honour to the chief of a trading party when it came to a post by making presents, many of which would be redistributed to the followers in due course. This practice, naturally, reinforced the prestige and influence of a chief in the eyes of his followers. However, another practice that the Bay men employed worked in the opposite direction. Often the trader would recognize as a "chief" anyone who headed a large party of would-be traders, creating an incentive among ambitious and commercially minded Native men to split off from their accustomed groups to form a body with which the company could deal. To some degree, this was a tool that an astute trader could use to try to keep a chief cooperating with the company — rather than "wasting" his efforts in warfare — for fear of losing followers and advantages if he went against the trader's desires. Because followership, in contrast to leadership, was always voluntary among Plains and woodlands groups, a chief who failed to provide adequately for his band might find his following eroding as a family here and there drew off and attached itself to another, presumably more successful, leader. To a degree that cannot be determined precisely, the Hudson's Bay Company practice worsened a tendency in some circumstances for bands to dissolve. Big Bear never experienced this problem as a result of the Bay's practices, but he would when dealing with another important institution during the last decade of his life.

Big Bear found other aspects of Plains political systems, especially those that demonstrated the traditional concerns about prestige and group harmony, more congenial. In his band, as throughout Plains society, his elevated status depended on the political institutions by which he was surrounded. As chief, he was aided in carrying out his political, diplomatic, and military functions by his criers, his caller, and his council.

The criers were prominent men whom the chief selected to act in his place when he was absent and to serve as intermediaries between him and individuals in the band who wanted something. They also carried out dangerous tasks such as enforcing peace if a disturbance broke out, as well as more pleasurable assignments such as announcing publicly that someone had made a gift to another band member. Although the criers received gifts of clothing and food from high-status men in the band, their office, which was often trying and sometimes even dangerous, conferred only status on them. Chief Big Bear's caller was an older man who also enjoyed receiving presents from others, but his job was related to considerations of prestige. When the chief wanted to have someone come to his lodge, the caller would announce the invitation loudly and publicly by calling out from its door. The way that he carried out his role reinforced the prestige of both the caller and those invited to Big Bear's side.

More important for political considerations than for status was the chief's council, which helped Big Bear to reach decisions on important questions. Senior men who enjoyed the respect of the community because of their attainments and skills constituted

FIGURE 5

Big Bear trading at Fort Pitt, c. 1884.

an informal advisory body to the chief. They would be called to Big Bear's lodge to discuss matters on which the chief was trying to reach conclusions. After he explained the issues to them, they would offer their views in a predetermined order, the youngest going first and the rest following in a kind of reverse-seniority order. When the oldest councillor had offered his advice and his reasons for it, Mistahimusqua would make a decision. It would be announced to the encampment by the chief's caller. The council was typical of political institutions used by most Aboriginal communities throughout the plains and woodlands in that its underlying purpose was to bring the group to a decision based, ideally, on consensus, or at least on wide consultation. While it was not true that everyone's opinion was as good as another's — only senior men were consulted, and the more senior the advisor, the more weight his counsel carried — the system of consultation with the council helped to ensure that Chief Big Bear was at least aware of community opinion while making a decision. The reasons for this procedure were mainly two: a decision taken after listening to the advice of experienced people would probably be better; and in Plains society, there were no coercive methods of enforcing decisions of the leadership. In a society that valued individual freedom, particularly in the young, Big Bear's leadership was effective to the degree that it enjoyed the support of his followers.

More ambiguous agents in the political system in Mistahimusqua's band were the Worthy Young Men and the warrior society. The former group, to which Big Bear himself had belonged when he was in his twenties and thirties, consisted of relatively young men who had distinguished themselves as fighters. Aside from enhanced status, the title conferred no advantages but in Plains society, status and prestige were extremely important considerations. In due course, most Worthy Young Men would be invited to join the warrior society, signifying that they had advanced to another plateau, one in which there were more outward signs of prestige. The society would have its own symbols, its own songs and dances, and its own lodge erected in the centre of the encampment by taking one pole from each tepee and skins for covers from tepees that had extras. Within the society, rank depended on the individual's prestige, and the most honoured member was known as the warrior chief, or war chief. The most important function of the warriors in peacetime was the enforcement of the rules governing the buffalo hunt to ensure that it was carried out in the most effective way possible. Warriors also had the responsibility of protecting the group when it was on the move, as Plains communities so frequently were for economic or military reasons. In peacetime, warriors were martial support for Big Bear's chieftainship; but when war broke out, the war chief effectively supplanted him as the decision maker for the community.

When Big Bear succeeded Black Powder in 1865, then, he took on a role whose burdens far outweighed its direct personal benefits. Now, in addition to looking out for his growing family, he was expected to make the decisions and provide the leadership, by example and otherwise, that would protect his community's well-being and guarantee its future. To carry out his tasks, he could rely on a senior men's council in political matters and on the warrior society for protection on the march and the policing of people's behaviour during the vitally important harvesting of the buffalo. His prestige was demonstrated publicly by the presence of his criers and his caller, who served as constant reminders of the central role of the chief in the lives of members of the band. However, his office also brought with it considerable burdens, both economic and social. In addition to having to make decisions about trading and hunting, Big Bear was expected to ensure that those who could not look after themselves were provided for by donations from successful hunters, himself most prominent among them. Finally, he was expected to maintain harmony between people who lived and worked in a sometimes claustrophobic atmosphere in which personal eccentricities, economic hardships, and base emotions such as envy and greed could threaten the peace at any moment.

THE COMING OF THE CANADIANS

For some time, Big Bear ensured that his leadership would be successful by attaching himself as a sort of dependent chief to a more powerful Cree leader. Among the bands in the Fort Pitt area, the leading man was Sweet Grass, who, like Big Bear, was not totally Cree. Sweet Grass, a Crow Indian who had merged with, and adopted the ways of, the Plains Cree, was older than Big Bear and well respected. For many years, Big Bear and his band followed Sweet Grass, benefiting from the older man's wise leadership. Judging by Big Bear's later career, one of the most important things that he absorbed while attached to Sweet Grass was the importance of peace. Throughout the pivotal decade of the 1860s, Sweet Grass worked energetically to try to end hostilities with the Blackfoot, to put an end to the destruction that had bedevilled both nations for so long. But peace eluded Sweet Grass, and both the older and younger leaders found numerous occasions to cooperate in raids into the territory controlled by the Blackfoot. On one important foray, they were attacked by a larger force of Blackfoot and almost wiped out. Such experiences presumably strengthened Big Bear's growing inclination to follow Sweet Grass's example — to seek an enduring peace.

Also threatening the peace and prosperity of Plains groups from 1865, when Big Bear became chief, were powerful if distant forces that would undermine the economic foundations of Plains culture within a generation. Farthest off was the American transcontinental railroad — "the fearsome fire wagons," as some Plains people called the mechanical monsters — that began construction in the later 1860s. When completed, the Union Pacific, and other railways that connected or competed with it, would bring large numbers of settlers and hunters to the high plains and prairie, thereby pressing yet further on the animal food resources of the western region. Big Bear himself did not see one of these monsters until the early 1880s, but they had begun to affect his way of life long before that encounter. Because the plains south and north of the international boundary were one huge economic and ecological system, the technological innovation and its social consequences would eventually make their impact on Plains groups along the North Saskatchewan as well.

Closer to home, parallel developments noticeable by the later 1860s also constituted a menace to the Plains way of life. The trickle of adventurers and settlers that had reached the area around the forks of the Red and Assiniboine Rivers in the 1850s was swelling noticeably by the time Big Bear became chief of his band. Their actual numbers posed no threat to either the Indian or mixed-blood peoples of Red River, let alone to the inhabitants of the Saskatchewan country hundreds of kilometres to the northwest, but what their arrival portended certainly did. The small groups from the east, who became known disapprovingly among Red River people as "the Canadian party," were an early indication of a growing desire in the Great Lakes basin to acquire the northwest and make it part of the eastern settlements. The land-hungry farmers and Toronto-based business interests of Upper Canada, the future province of Ontario, wanted to put an end to the Hudson's Bay Company control of the northwest and acquire the region's enormous agricultural potential for themselves. Local political obstacles prevented them from pursuing this goal very successfully until they joined with other colonies of Britain to form the Dominion of Canada in July 1867. Not only did the new state have the resources to take over and develop the northwest, but one of Ontario's conditions for participating in the new political arrangement was that the dominion would pursue acquisition of the west forthwith.

Canada soon began asking how it might acquire whatever rights the Bay had in the west; at the same time, it was taking steps that already suggested its ownership. As early as 1868, a road-building crew was at work in the region between the northwest angle of Lake of the Woods and the flatlands to the east of Red River, much to the annoyance of local Ojibwa groups, who told the road builders they had no right to be working in their territories without permission.

Canada's aggressive interest in what the British government called Rupert's Land obviously had ominous implications for the Native groups throughout the region. The Hudson's Bay Company charter of 1670 had presumed to give the company a trading monopoly and hazily defined property and political rights over all the lands drained by rivers flowing into James Bay and Hudson Bay. The company had not shown much interest in exerting control of the land itself; being a trading company, it was interested more in commerce than in settlement. And for Plains traders such as Black Powder and Big Bear, the Bay meant a source of manufactured goods in trade, not a force that threatened possession of their territory or control over their decision making. However, the Hudson's Bay Company had fostered the creation of the Selkirk Settlement from 1812 onward in the valley of the Red River with little concern for the land rights of the Assiniboine and Saulteaux peoples of the region. The company had also created a rudimentary, fragile government structure called the Council of Assiniboia, but it, like the trading monopoly, was not an effective instrument by the 1850s.

For Big Bear and other Native people throughout the western region, the biggest concern arose from doubt about the future role of the Hudson's Bay Company. How might it change as a result of Canadian expansion, and what would be the consequences for trade? In the short run, the question was whether the Bay would disappear entirely from the region; in the longer run, concern arose from the likelihood that large-scale settlement would disrupt the traditional hunting life of the Plains people. No one could imagine change so great that the buffalo-based economy would be drastically harmed, but everyone could understand that the coming of Canadians to farm would interfere with the seasonal migrations and extensive use of the land and its resources by the Cree, Blackfoot, and other Plains peoples.

When Canadian rule did come to the west in 1869–70, it appeared both less and more threatening than had been feared. It was less unsettling for the Plains groups that traded with the Hudson's Bay Company, because the transfer of its interest in the region did not lead to the disappearance of it and its trading posts. As a result of the negotiations between Canada, the United Kingdom, and the Bay, the company retained five percent of the lands in its former area, with those lands situated around the posts it would continue to operate. Big Bear's band could expect to continue their regular trade at Fort Carlton or, as was by now more usual, Fort Pitt farther west on the North Saskatchewan River.

However, the Bay's surrender of its rights in the west to the Dominion of Canada was seriously negative in other ways. The first adverse point was that the Bay had acted throughout the difficult negotiations as though it, not the Aboriginal peoples, was the rightful owner of the lands. The second was that Canada showed absolutely no concern to discuss its plans with, and gain the agreement of, either Indians or mixed-blood peoples in Rupert's Land. By ignoring the Métis, Canada provoked a resistance by armed men under the leadership of Louis Riel in Red River over the autumn–winter of 1869–70, a standoff that ended only when the dominion negotiated terms for creating the Province of Manitoba that were satisfactory to Riel and his advisors. Throughout the strained months of the Red River Resistance, Canada showed no inclination to consult the Indian peoples, even though the Métis provisional government that Riel set up mentioned their interests in one of the lists of demands that it put forward during the crisis. The actions that Canada both took and failed to take between 1868 and 1870 did not augur well for the future of relations between the dominion and the Cree and other First Nations of the plains and parklands to the west of the new province called Manitoba.

Far away in the Saskatchewan country, Big Bear and other leaders would learn in due course of the Canadians' strange and provocative behaviour. However, even before they heard about the Canadian government's peculiar ways, they were treated to a threatening action by another group of Canadians. In 1866, a Methodist missionary who had come from Ontario to minister to the Native peoples of Alberta struck a symbolic blow at Plains

FIGURE 6

Mistahimusqua, armed.

people and their livelihood. The Methodists, who were distinctive for their habit of referring to one another as "brother," had come to the North Saskatchewan in the 1830s. (The other major Christian group, the Roman Catholics, who referred to their leaders as "fathers," had begun to develop missions in the Canadian Shield country to the north of the Plains region from the 1840s onward.) Just a year after Big Bear became chief, one of these Methodist brothers challenged a spiritual observance of the Plains Cree. According to his son John, who also served as a Methodist missionary in the west, the Reverend George McDougall stole a monument the buffalo hunters regarded as particularly important. The stone, apparently a meteorite, weighed 135 kilograms and rung "like steel when struck with a piece of iron." McDougall knew that Plains people believed it had been placed on the plains by the Creator. "For ages," he noted, "the tribes of Blackfeet and Crees have gathered their clans to pay homage to this wonderful manitoo." Nonetheless, a converted Indian took the stone and carted it to McDougall's mission at Victoria; it would later end up on the grounds of the Methodist university in Ontario. McDougall reported to his church that the theft angered the Native population, especially the spiritual leaders: "They declared that sickness, war, and decrease of buffalo would follow the sacrilege." Happily, he noted, their prediction proved inaccurate in the summer of 1868, for thousands of buffalo came to the Saskatchewan country and filled the larders of Cree and other hunters.

For Big Bear and his following, the bountiful hunt of 1868 would prove to be the end of the good years for them and all Plains peoples. Big Bear personally had found the years since he had assumed the leadership after Black Powder's death fruitful. In all, he had three wives and seven children. With Sayos, his first and most favoured wife, he had had four children, two girls and two boys. Some of their children, such as the older daughter, were themselves married, in her case to Lone Man, who became very close to Big Bear. His oldest son, Twin Wolverine, was also married now and raising a family. This distinguished him from the second son, Imasees, who was still regularly engaged in warfare as befitted a young, unmarried fellow. Within a few years, however, Imasees would settle down to married life, too, and help to produce the grandchildren who gave such pleasure to Big Bear and his extended family. If young soldiers such as Imasees were giving up raids on the Blackfoot, older and wiser leaders such as Big Bear knew that it was largely because enormous pressures were finally forcing warring Plains peoples to make peace. The diseases that wiped out thousands in 1870 were certainly one major factor. So, too, was the growing concern about a possible threat from the Euro-Canadians and Americans who were increasingly coming into the country. Big Bear no doubt approved of the course of action that Sweet Grass and some other senior chiefs took in 1871 when they approached the far-off Dominion of Canada about entering into an agreement with the queen's government in Ottawa. According to treaty commissioner Alexander Morris's account, Sweet Grass said in his message to the queen's representative that the chiefs had "heard our lands were sold and we did not like it; we don't want to sell our lands; it is our property, and no one has a right to sell them." He and others were worried about the depletion of game: "we want you to pity us. We want cattle, tools, agricultural implements, and assistance in everything when we come to settle — our country is no longer able to support us." Sweet Grass also asked for government help in preventing Americans from coming into their lands "and giving . . . ammunition and arms to our enemies the Blackfeet." He noted that the Cree had just made peace with their ancient enemies to the southwest, and he suggested that Canada should enter into an agreement with them, too. "We invite you to come and see us and to speak with us. If you can't come yourself, send some one in your place." Both the peace treaty with the Blackfoot Confederacy and the overture that Sweet Grass and several other chiefs made to Canada were indications that they and others recognized the Cree, like Plains peoples generally, stood at a very ominous transitional point in the 1870s.

HUNTING THE BUFFALO

Until they could reap the benefits of peace and negotiate a relationship with Canada that would protect and assist them, Big Bear and other Plains leaders carried on in their traditional manner as best they could. As long as the spirits willed the buffalo to come into their hunting territories, the summer hunt remained the focal point of their annual routine. According to Robert Jefferson, an Englishman who came to the North Saskatchewan country to teach on Red Pheasant's reserve in 1878, the annual buffalo hunt was central to the lives of the Cree. Once a sufficient number of them assembled in the summer, the first thing they did was appoint a group of "soldiers," or police, for the hunt. These young men were responsible for maintaining discipline in the hunting camp, something absolutely vital to the safety and success of the hunters and their companions. When the pursuit of bison took them into or close to enemy territory, firm control over movement and fires was essential to minimize the chances of detection. While scouts were out trying to locate a herd, the maintenance of as much quiet and stillness as possible was also important to avoid alerting and frightening off the prey. Once the actual running of the animals was about to begin, the soldiers regulated the mounted hunters to ensure that none took an unfair advantage over the rest.

Chief Big Bear knew that discipline had to be maintained, because even a large and apparently disorganized hunting camp had its predetermined social order and rules of behaviour. When his band was in pursuit of the buffalo herds, it pitched its hunting camp in a large circle of tepees, with the lodges of related families usually found in a cluster in the congregation. The circle of tents could also serve as a makeshift corral within which the horses could be tethered for security, in case a scout had brought Big Bear intelligence of the presence of a marauding enemy party, which would make picketing them out on the nearby prairie too dangerous. The camp also had a special place for the soldiers' tent, as well as for the tepees of the several chiefs, whose dwellings were pitched in the centre of the encampment. Children and dogs roamed about the camp at will, and their commotion and noise added to the misleading impression of near chaos that a camp sometimes gave.

Critically important were the roles of the women, who had a long list of tasks on which the comfort of the community depended. While camped, the mothers and their daughters looked after food preparation and other domestic arrangements. When it was time to move in search of the buffalo or to escape attack, they had much of the work of packing up, loading travois, and keeping an eye on children and dogs. Even a chief's wives, such as Sayos and the others, were subject to this routine.

For the men, their roles were mainly as hunters and protectors against enemy attack. Chief Big Bear did not have to make many decisions when his band was actually out on the plains on the hunt, because the warriors provided most of the directions in the process of locating, hunting down, and harvesting the buffalo. When a herd had been detected by outriders and the soldiers had finally given the signal that the hunt was on, the men swung into action on their horses. They were lined up by the soldiers and sent off in the direction of the herd, Jefferson observed, "at a pace regulated by the slowest" in order to ensure that all would have a reasonably equal chance. Once they got close enough to their prey that the slow-mounted were not seriously disadvantaged, the rush was on. Each hunter kneed his steed on urgently, trying to get among the herd before the beasts could take flight and race off.

Once the hunters reached the buffalo, they set about killing as many as swiftly as they could. The weapon could be a newfangled instrument such as a firearm, usually the fairly inaccurate muzzle-loaders still in use in the 1870s, though a few of the new and more accurate rifles were available. But Big Bear and many other hunters thought that the traditional bow and arrow still worked best. Selecting another arrow from the quiver and firing it was an easier and faster operation when thundering along amid the herd than trying to reload a musket. Jefferson said that the Cree were efficient with bow and arrow, sometimes "sending an arrow completely through the body of a buffalo. The arrows were carried in a quiver on the back, in such a position that the bearer, by throwing his right hand just over the left shoulder, could grasp an arrow. The drawing of the arrow, the fitting on the bowstring and the discharging are three movements merged into one, so perfect is their continuity." Each hunter's arrows were distinctive, with some feature of the feathers or decoration that indicated the maker and owner. This was important to mark the kill as belonging to a particular individual. For those who used a firearm to drop a buffalo, it was necessary to pause briefly and throw down some marker to claim the trophy later. Whether the hunter used a Winchester rifle, muzzle-loading musket, or arrows, he pounded along beside the herd until either he had downed a sufficient number of the shaggy beasts or they had succeeded in getting away. The buffalo was large, and its eyesight was not good at a distance, but when in motion, especially when alarmed, it could move with amazing swiftness for an animal its size.

Once the hunt was completed, the hunters, with Chief Big Bear riding as just another member of the hunting party, returned to the camp to enjoy their well-earned praise and get the rest of the population to start on the work of butchering the kill. With carts and travois, most of the camp's population accompanied the hunters back to where the animals had been killed, and the laborious process of butchering began, as Jefferson witnessed:

> First, the head of the dead animal is twisted round under its shoulder so as to support the carcass nearly fair on its back. The feet are dislocated and skinning proceeds on the side most exposed. The head is then turned the other way and . . . tilted slightly to that side, so that the hide may be easily cut from the backbone. The loose skin is then spread out, that the flesh may not touch the ground. The meat along each side of the backbone is cut away clean, to secure the

long sinew intact. Next the short sinews under the shoulderblade. Then the legs are taken off and the ribs chopped from the backbone. Over goes the carcass again, and all this is repeated. All the severed parts are thrown into the conveyance, leaving the insides and head on the hide to be picked over. The tongue, liver and the "book" part of the stomach are then taken. The tongue is a tit-bit, while the liver and "book" are eaten raw, in which condition they are accounted great delicacies.

Special care was taken not to damage the hide, because the processed skin had both many uses among the band and marketability with the white traders. With the skinning and large-scale butchering complete, the workers made their way back to the camp for the rest of the work.

When the spoils of the hunt had been transferred to the camp, they came under the exclusive care of Sayos and the other women. The men had hunted the animals, and virtually everyone had been involved in the preliminary butchering and transporting, but the rest of the important work was the responsibility of the women. Their skills in processing the flesh and other products of the animal were extremely important to everyone's well-being. The first task was to get the edible flesh dried and the other parts prepared for later attention. The sinews were cleaned and hung to dry; the skin was stretched on a frame while it was still wet. Then attention turned to the meat, which was cut into long strips, preferably very thin strips, which were strung on sticks and dried over a smoky fire. When the meat was properly dried, it would be stored for later use. Immediately, the bones were set aside, and efforts were devoted to the hide. Every scrap of flesh was picked, pummelled, and finally scraped from the skin using a piece of bone or a metal block fashioned from some obsolete manufactured item, such as a gun barrel. If time and circumstances permitted, the women then tanned the hide by scraping off all hair and making it soft and malleable by repeated applications of a mixture of grease, liver, and brain. The skin,

FIGURE 7

Buffalo pound.

thus treated, would be pulled and folded and kneaded until, after many hours of hard manual labour, it became soft and pliable. If conditions did not allow the lengthy tanning process to be undertaken on the spot, the dried skin would be folded carefully and stored away for some future opportunity. The tanned skin could be used with others to make a new tepee, turned into clothes, or traded for other goods. The bones of the buffalo would be cracked and broken with stones, then boiled to release their fat, a Plains delicacy.

In Big Bear's and other communities, other methods of hunting were sometimes used: the buffalo pound and the buffalo jump. The advantage of the pound was that it could be used in winter or summer, but its drawback was that it depended on the availability of a bush or forest to work. A man who could make a pound, or surround, and ensure that buffalo were secured by means of it was someone of enormous prestige and power in his community. It was believed that the poundmaker had a special relationship with the spirit of the buffalo that made the animals give themselves up to be captured and slaughtered by the people. The pound would be constructed near the bottom of a down grade, and it consisted of a circular fence more than two metres high and twenty-five or more metres in diameter. It had an opening at the up-slope end, and the drive lane that led to it was lined with brush fences that guided the buffalo toward their fate. Beyond the brush-lined lane, members of the group would station themselves as inconspicuously as possible in a funnel-like arrangement that might stretch hundreds of metres away from the lane. The poundmaker and other horsemen would attempt to induce a herd to run toward the pound by riding close to the flank of the herd. As the animals got closer to the drive lane, individual people would pop up and wave a blanket at the buffalo if they seemed to be heading away from the preordained course. Once they were in the enclosure, their exit was blocked by a group of people waving blankets at them; they were then shot down by the men.

The buffalo jump resembled the pound insofar as the hunters

FIGURE 8
Buffalo jump.

stampeded a herd through a set course dictated by both horsemen and people concealed along the side. In the case of the buffalo jump, however, the run ended at a slope — ideally a precipice with a slight rise a short distance in front of it — over which the animals tumbled to their immediate death. That buffalo had poor eyesight, forelegs shorter than their hind limbs, and great mass made it difficult for the herd to halt its progress even when the lead animals finally saw the drop before them. Either in a buffalo pound or at the foot of a buffalo jump, the animals received the same fate as their kin shot on the open prairie. The skinning and butchering methods from that point on were all the same.

The buffalo was the foundation of the economy and way of life of all the Plains peoples, including Big Bear, Sweet Grass, and the Blackfoot who had so recently been their enemies. The flesh of the animal, of course, was a vital source of protein-rich sustenance, and, when dried and made into pemmican by adding grease and berries and pounding the lot into a congealed substance, it could serve as either stored food for the family or a trade item that Hudson's Bay Company traders were anxious to get. The Methodist missionary George McDougall noted in 1869 that the spring hunt of the Cree people around his mission at Victoria had involved one thousand people, killed five thousand buffalo, and yielded "one hundred and twenty thousand pounds [fifty-five thousand kilograms] of dried meat." Even for the highly carnivorous Plains people in Big Bear's following, such a bountiful harvest would probably carry them through the lean months of winter.

Other buffalo parts served important purposes. Skins were potential trade items, but most likely those that Big Bear's people took were needed for lodge coverings, clothing, and utensils in all but the most productive years of hunting. Sinews were used to tie or lash items together. The bones, once they were cleaned of marrow and grease, could be put to use as spoons and other utensils. The horns were useful as drinking vessels or, when lined carefully with noncombustible material, to carry live coals with which to make a fire at the next campsite. When the Plains peoples were out on the prairie and far from firewood in the bush country, they could use the dry manure from the vast buffalo herds for their fires. And, significantly, the buffalo had an important place in their spiritual lives, one that reflected the animal's centrality to the Plains civilization. The skull of the buffalo served as something like an altar during the religious ceremony known as the Sun Dance among the Blackfoot and the Thirst Dance among the Cree. Buffalo tongues were an important ingredient in the rituals of these dance ceremonies, which took place in the late spring, and one of the most important religious fraternities was known as the Horn Society.

Even someone insensitive enough to steal a monument of special significance to the Saskatchewan-country people could appreciate how essential the buffalo were to the Cree and other Plains peoples. In 1875, in one of the last letters he wrote from his prairie mission field, George McDougall tried to explain to an eastern friend the importance of the buffalo:

> Just suppose that all supplies were cut off from Montreal: all factories closed because there was nothing to manufacture; the markets forsaken because there was nothing to sell; in addition to this neither building material nor fuel to be obtained; how sad would be the condition of the tens of thousands of your great city! Now, the situation of these prairie tribes is exactly analogous to this state. For ages they have lived upon the buffalo; with its pelt they make their wigwams; wrapped in the robe of the buffalo they feared not the cold; from the flesh of this wild ox they made their pemmican and dried meat; while they possessed his sinews they needed no stronger thread; from its ribs they manufactured sleighs.... The manure of the buffalo is all the fuel they had — in a word they were totally dependent on the buffalo....

The Methodist missionary understood better than most almost all the important uses to which the Plains Cree and Blackfoot put the buffalo. Perhaps it is not surprising, though, that the man who applauded the theft in 1866 of the meteorite — an "idol" he called it, scoffing at the predictions of the "conjurors" that its removal meant pestilence, destruction, and disappearance of the buffalo — never understood or mentioned the religious role of the buffalo.

TREATY TIME

Big Bear and his mentor, Chief Sweet Grass, feared that the buffalo would not be available long in sufficient quantities, whether the reason was offending the spirit of the buffalo by removing one of the monuments to it or simply overhunting. It was true that 1868 and 1869 had been particularly good years for hunting the beasts along the North Saskatchewan and the lands to the south of the river. However, there were signs of increasing change and pressure that created worries not even the peace treaty between the Blackfoot and their northeastern foes could lighten. The highly efficient Plains communication system, the moccasin telegraph that had carried word of the Métis resistance in 1869–70 to the Cree along the North Saskatchewan, brought Big Bear and Sweet Grass news of other, even more disturbing developments. They learned that a small but steady stream of agricultural settlers was flowing onto the plains from an eastern territory called Ontario. In 1873, some Saulteaux and Dakota around a settlement that the newcomers called Portage la Prairie warned the settlers not to cut any more firewood without the permission of the Native peoples. From the same eastern point of origin, apparently, came a red-coated police force in 1874. These soldiers of the queen, North West Mounted Police they said they were, did help their Blackfoot neighbours by driving out the whisky peddlers who had been such a destructive influence in southern Alberta and the Cypress Hills area, but they were also an ominous sign that another power thought it had the right to put its soldiers in the Natives' buffalo country.

The response of the great queen mother to the message about entering negotiations that Sweet Grass and some other chiefs had sent in 1871 was puzzling and not all that reassuring. The queen's Canadian government had sent a message through a man with the title of lieutenant-governor of Manitoba that the queen did not want their part of the plains for settlement right away, but she might before too long. Even stranger was that this Lieutenant-Governor Adams Archibald added that their queen mother wanted them to act like "good subjects," whatever that meant. What was clear was that slowly and surely more of the queen's other good subjects, Canadians, were coming for one purpose or another.

For Big Bear and others, the early years of the 1870s were both the high point of development and the edge of a slope to destruction. Their society was intact, and their economy, especially in years such as 1868 when the spirit of the buffalo helped so generously, was well developed. The problems of disease and heavy pressure on the buffalo had recently led them to conclude a peace with the Blackfoot Confederacy to the southwest. Although there were certainly challenges aplenty to Plains peoples in these years, the Cree were far from being a defeated or even a cowed nation. They would have to deal with a drastic decline in their main source of sustenance, but they were a dynamic and resourceful community who had responded to, and overcome, major challenges before. They certainly were not ready to accept control by another people or complete loss of their territory. What had the queen's representative, this Archibald, meant when he urged them to conduct themselves like good subjects of the queen mother?

For Chief Big Bear, the 1870s seemed to be a good time on the personal level at least. He was growing in reputation among his own people and other bands, and his family was maturing and happy. However, there were also times when the buffalo, strangely, did not come to the Saskatchewan country and hunger visited the lodges. What was to become of the Cree if the buffalo became less numerous? (No one ever dreamed that they could go away almost completely.) For a father and chief such as Big Bear, at the height of his reputation and power at the age of fifty, it was certainly a worrisome question.

One morning, on 14 August 1874, Big Bear was surprised to see the Hudson's Bay Company man arrive at his camp. Even though it was summer and Factor William McKay would not have had a lot of trading to do at his home base at Fort Pitt, it was strange to see him so far out on the plains, a full seven days from his trading post on the North Saskatchewan. As promising as it was intriguing, he was accompanied by four carts loaded with packages and barrels. And why did their old friend McKay say that he brought them a message from the queen mother? As McKay later reported to Richard Hardisty, he told Big Bear that her government in Ottawa was anxious that the Plains Cree bands in the upper Saskatchewan country know why she had sent policemen into their country that summer. Big Bear listened carefully as the emissary from the queen — whose orders in fact originated with Lieutenant-Governor Alexander Morris in Winnipeg — explained that the North West Mounted Police had been sent into the west not to threaten the Cree but to protect them and other Native groups from wrongdoers, such as the American whisky traders who had been making life hellish for the Blackfoot. The queen did not want her police to cause any problems, and she did not expect her Cree "children" to help the Mounties in any fighting in which they might become embroiled as they worked to clear the plains of troublesome intruders.

Big Bear understood that portion of McKay's explanation well enough, though another part of the message puzzled him. The Bay man also said that the queen had sent some of her soldiers who, along with "a party of American soldiers," were "to mark out the line between Her Territories and those of the United States so that Her Indian & White subjects might know where the lands of the Queen" began. Less puzzling, but more revealing, was something that happened at the end of the visit. Before McKay moved on to visit the camps of several other Cree chiefs, including that of Sweet Grass, he distributed a number of presents to reinforce in a material way what he had been telling Big Bear's people about the goodwill that had motivated the queen, her soldiers, and her police. Gifts of ammunition, powder, tea, sugar, tobacco, knives, and clay pipes were warmly accepted in almost all of the sixty-five tents in Big Bear's camp. Two families, noted McKay, "objected to receive the present, stating it was given them as a bribe to facilitate a future treaty."

Not all the Plains Cree were pleased that this thing calling itself "Canada" was finally taking proper notice that the lands its representatives were more and more often invading were controlled by Big Bear and other leaders. This was a more substantial response than the one that Sweet Grass and the other chiefs had received to their 1871 overture about negotiating a treaty. Perhaps this Canada was reacting to the signs of resistance by a variety of groups, such as the Saulteaux around Portage la Prairie. The Dominion of Canada had already found out to its sorrow what would happen if it attempted to take over territory without negotiating with the Indigenous population of the area. Prior to the Red River Resistance of 1869–70, Prime Minister John A. Macdonald and his government had thought that purchasing the Hudson's Bay Company rights to the vast territory called Rupert's Land gave them sufficient title to move in and establish themselves. However, Louis Riel and the Métis had proved by force of arms that this was not the case. And, if that was not proof enough of the necessity to bargain with the Indigenous inhabitants of the west in advance of settlement, opposition to road-building crews and military forces in the region between Lake of the Woods and Red River both before and after the resistance underlined the lesson.

Closer to Big Bear's world, some Cree chiefs also made their resentment of Canada's unauthorized intrusions known. In 1875, for example, Mistawasis, a chief of the Willow Cree near Fort Carlton, ordered his soldiers to stop and warn off a group of workmen who were putting trees without branches into the ground. The strangers, when Mistawasis's men advised them that they were unlawfully invading Cree lands, said that they were building the telegraph line for the Dominion of Canada. Their purpose was only slightly less mysterious to these Plains Cree than that of a party of scientists from the Geological Survey of Canada who were also ordered out of Cree lands by some of Mistawasis's soldiers in 1875. By the middle years of the 1870s, then, the government of Canada knew from protests that its agents were encountering in northwestern Ontario and in the Saskatchewan country that it would have to conclude treaties with the peoples of the western plains if it was to make its control of the region secure enough to permit peaceful agricultural settlement.

Big Bear had no way of knowing that Canada, as it turned to the task of making treaties with the western nations, did so against the background of a long tradition and several assistants on which it could call for guidance and support in negotiating pacts. From Britain, the dominion had inherited the practice of taking land from Aboriginal peoples through a representative of the crown, a custom that had been established by the Royal Proclamation of 1763 and followed imperfectly but often ever since. Most of the lands in what would become southern Ontario had been obtained from the Mississauga by negotiation between 1780 and 1830. The earliest treaties had involved lump-sum payments of money and goods to the Native peoples in return for what the government took to be title to their lands. After the War of 1812, the authorities shifted to a somewhat different style of treaty making. Henceforth, the compensation that Indian negotiators would get for their lands would take the form of small annual payments, or annuities, which probably seemed congenial to them because they resembled the annual "presents" that the crown had given to them during the period of close military alliance that stretched from the Seven Years' War (1756–63) to the War of 1812 (1812–14). In this manner, the government of what eventually became Canada's largest province developed a tradition of negotiating peaceful access to Native lands in advance of agricultural settlement.

Canadian practice, however, was neither altruistic nor consistent. The motivation behind negotiating for lands rather than seeking to conquer Native landholders was to avoid destructive and costly wars. In the decades after the Royal Proclamation of 1763, Britain used negotiations for land in large part to remain on good terms with Indian nations during an era when her thirteen colonies were in a restive mood. Later, when treaties were made with the Mississauga north of the lower Great Lakes, the primary reason was that negotiation was less costly and bloody than warfare, especially when British troops and colonial militia were few and faced a potential Aboriginal force that greatly outnumbered them. When the end of the War of 1812 ushered in peace between the Americans and the British, the crown became less concerned with conciliating Native landowners and more high-handed in its dealings with them. Especially between 1820 and 1860 in the future Ontario, when large-scale immigration swamped the Indigenous population, there were increasingly frequent departures from respect for Native land rights.

Nor were the British and colonials always faithful to the tradition that required them to negotiate through the crown for Native land. A deviation occurred in the second decade of the nineteenth century, when Lord Selkirk of Red River only got around to negotiating a treaty with the local people several years after his colony had been established at the forks of the Red and Assiniboine Rivers. The Scottish lord's willingness to negotiate the Selkirk Treaty in 1817 might have had something to do with a desire to remain on good terms with the Saulteaux and others, given the clash between Selkirk settlers and Métis at Seven Oaks in 1816 that had resulted in the deaths of a number of the former. Also typical of the colonists' inconsistent adherence to official policy concerning Aboriginal lands was the background to the Robinson Treaties of 1850. In the case of these pacts, which obtained peaceful access to large areas of land northeast of Lake Huron and north of Lake Superior, treaty making only occurred because and after the local Native population took exception to unauthorized explorations by mining companies in their lands. When Ojibwa groups threatened the miners, the colonial government sent a negotiator north to conclude the Robinson Huron and Robinson Superior Treaties. One feature of the treaties that would stand as a precedent for later negotiations in the west was a provision that guaranteed the Ojibwa signers the right to continue to hunt and fish throughout the tract surrendered by treaty as long as settlement and other non-Native economic uses did not require the lands. Even this apparently benevolent provision illustrated the self-interested approach that the government took to negotiations, for treaty commissioner William B. Robinson reported that he agreed to this guarantee to ensure that the Ojibwa would not claim later that they had a right to financial support from the government.

As Canada turned to making treaties in the west following the acquisition of Rupert's Land from the Hudson's Bay Company, it had a long, if intermittent, tradition of treaty making to which it could turn for instruction. Since the 1780s especially, it had negotiated for lands with Indigenous populations, including some of the groups in the Red River area. By the middle of the nineteenth century, it had established a pattern in its treaties: Native groups surrendered large tracts of land in return for small initial payments, annual compensation, and a guarantee of a right to continue using their lands in traditional economic fashion until settlement made that impossible. Sometimes, as in the case of the Robinson Treaties, part of the deal was the creation of what the government called "reserves" for the Native groups. This practice was both a continuation of something that had developed earlier independent of treaty making and a recognition that Native negotiators desired tracts of land they could be certain were theirs. Many of these elements of treaty making would surface again when Canada began making the western treaties in the 1870s.

As McKay's visit to Big Bear's camp in August 1874 illustrated, when Canada began to make overtures to the Plains nations in the 1870s, it had more than tradition on which to rely for help; it could also count on the assistance of several groups influential among the Plains peoples in particular. One agency that lent a measure of support was the Hudson's Bay Company, the European presence with which most Plains groups were familiar and from whose traders they had learned the ways of the newcomers. The Bay men were not especially pleased with Canada, for they thought that the dominion had driven a hard bargain when it arranged through the United Kingdom to obtain land rights for £300,000 and one-twentieth of the lands, to be chosen around existing Bay posts. However disgruntled the Bay might have been at the time of transfer, its representatives in the west recognized that Canada henceforth would be the controlling power and that Ottawa might be useful to the company in the future. Accordingly, Bay men, who were often liked and respected by Native leaders, usually supported the treaty-making process when asked for advice.

Less influential, but also less equivocal in their support of Canada's treaty-making strategy in the 1870s, were a small number of Christian missionaries in the west. The Methodists and Roman Catholics, both of whom had been planted in the future Manitoba and regions to the west for some time, were especially supportive. The Methodist John McDougall lent his support for Treaty Seven in southern Alberta in 1877, as did the venerable oblate priest Father Albert Lacombe. Another oblate missionary, Father Constantine Scollen, was present at the making of Treaty Six at Fort Carlton in 1876. In part, the clerics' approval of the treaty process was based on their loyalty to Canada as a British colony, but there were other reasons as well. Especially when it came to negotiating treaties in the plains and parklands in 1874, 1876, and 1877, the missionaries were keen to see the pacts signed because they were increasingly anxious about the Natives' economic future. Causing them concern was the rapid dwindling of the buffalo in these years. For anxious missionaries, treaties, reserves, and assistance with settling down to agriculture were perceived as a potential alternative to the vanishing resource. Of course, Indians who were settled on reserves and practising agriculture were also seen by missionaries as better prospects for successful, permanent conversion to Christianity. The evangelists' support of treaty making was based both on genuine concern for Plains peoples' well-being and on a desire to advance the missionary agenda.

The final instrument that Ottawa had at its disposal as it moved to conclude treaties with the western nations was the one whose presence McKay was most anxious to explain to Big Bear in 1874. The North West Mounted Police (NWMP) force, which Ottawa created in 1873 and dispatched to the west the following year, was designed to establish effective Canadian control of the region, especially by wiping out the whisky traders in southern Alberta. Prime Minister Macdonald had recognized for years that the creation of a federal police force would be essential, both to ensure peaceful relations between Natives and newcomers and to assert Canadian title effectively for the benefit of Canada's southern neighbours. The murder of a score of Assiniboine men and the abuse of some of their wives by drunken wolf hunters — an episode that became known as the Cypress Hills Massacre — during the winter of 1872–73 merely underlined the urgency of getting a force into the field. From the beginning, the planning behind the dispatch of the NWMP included the idea that they would wear scarlet tunics, for it was believed that the Cree, Blackfoot, and other nations of the west would identify red-coated police with the British military tradition to which many of them had been allied in years past. Even if that association did not occur, red coats would distinguish the queen's policemen from the hated "long knives," the blue-uniformed American cavalry forces with whom many groups had had brushes.

The early activities of the mounted police after their arrival in the southwestern plains in 1874 confirmed the government's strategy and helped to win support for negotiating treaties soon afterward. The horsemen did succeed in cleaning out the "whisky forts" at which distilled poison had been traded to the Blackfoot and others with devastating results. More generally, they would prove to be a buffer in subsequent years between Indigenous peoples and immigrant farmers who did not always understand or respect the property rights of the Native population. Relations between police and Native peoples were so good during the first decade of the red coats' presence in the west, according to R.C. Macleod, that the NWMP did not fire a shot in anger at a Métis or Indian until 1885. This early success was reflected in the attitudes that some of the Native negotiators expressed during the making of the treaties. At Blackfoot Crossing in 1877, Crowfoot, an influential Blackfoot chief, referred directly to the role of Canadian law while supporting the proposed treaty. "If the Police had not come to the country, where would we [all be] now?" he asked. "Bad men and whiskey were killing us so fast that very few, indeed, of us would have been left to-day. The Police have protected us as the feathers of the bird protect it from the frosts of winter." More significantly, as treaty commissioner Alexander Morris later reported Crowfoot's speech, the chief went on to say, "I wish them all good, and trust that all our hearts will increase in goodness from this time forward. I am satisfied. I will sign the treaty." Big Bear's people had not been as directly affected by the whisky peddlers as the Blackfoot had been, but the chief knew from McKay and others that the problems these merchants of liquid death had created were part of the reason the queen had sent her red coats to the plains.

"I WILL ACCEPT THE QUEEN'S HAND"

Even though Canada had tradition, the Bay, missionaries, and the mounted police on its side as it attempted to conclude treaties, it did not carry the day easily or completely. In fact, it was remarkable how strong resistance was from the various groups that Canada approached to negotiate agreements. The dominion initiated treaty-making efforts among the Ojibwa of northwestern Ontario in 1871, because that was the quarter from which resistance to the activities of road builders and the passage of militiamen had come in 1869 and 1870. However, the demands of the Native negotiators were so great that agreement could

FIGURE 9

Negotiations at Stone Fort (Winnipeg), 1871.

not be reached with them until 1873, in what became known as the North West Angle Treaty (Treaty Three). Indicative of Ojibwa thinking was the chief who told a startled government negotiator that Canada should indicate which parcels of land it sought to acquire by agreement, leaving the Native population in control of the remainder. It took considerable time for Ottawa's representative to convince the Natives that the government would make treaty only on the basis that the Ojibwa surrender all the land except for small pockets, which would become known as reserves.

Another example of the difficulties that Ottawa encountered was the 1871 negotiation of the Stone Fort Treaty, or Treaty One, in Manitoba. At these parleys, according to Jean Friesen, Native negotiators had a lengthy list of demands:

> We want all the children to be clothed with fine clothes. . . . Whenever an Indian wants to settle, a house is to be put up for him fully furnished, and a plough with all its accompaniments of cattle etc. complete, is to be given him. We want buggies for the chiefs, councillors and braves to show their dignity. Each man is to be supplied with whatever he sees for hunting. . . . Each Indian settling on the reserve is to be free from taxes!

As Friesen explains, the Native negotiators made these demands because their sense of balance and mutuality justified them in their own minds: they were opening a vast territory to newcomers, and the least the strangers could do was to treat them generously and with dignity.

The efficient communications system of the prairies spread word to the Cree and Blackfoot of what transpired during the making of the first treaties in the early 1870s. Big Bear and the other chiefs would have heard how government negotiators faced various obstacles in reaching agreements with the Assiniboine and Saulteaux. When Treaty One was concluded in 1871, Ottawa's man could only get agreement by conceding verbally a number of items that he did not have authorization to include in the treaty. (This was only after the Indigenous peoples' representatives tried and failed to get agreement that they would retain control over about two-thirds of Manitoba.) Aboriginal negotiators successfully pressed for oral promises of clothing for head men of a band, farm stock, and implements for farming. These "outside promises," as the government euphemistically called them, would prove to be a source of friction between Natives and Ottawa until the federal authority finally conceded four years later that they were part of the agreement and made good on them. In 1874, another problem manifested itself at negotiations of the Qu'Appelle Treaty, or Treaty Four. Saulteaux negotiators in particular were affronted that talks were to take place at the Hudson's Bay Company post, because they regarded the Bay as the illegal recipient of Canadian payments for western lands. Preliminary discussions were protracted and angry, as Native representatives insisted that Canada hand over the monies that had improperly gone to the Bay. Only after much wrangling was it possible to move on to discuss the substance of the treaty.

The other difficulty that Canada encountered in negotiating the treaties was that Native bargainers tended to build on the achievements of their predecessors, gradually increasing the concessions they extracted from Ottawa's hard-pressed agents. For example, the difficult negotiations that culminated in Treaty Three in 1873 secured for the Native bargainers significant improvements in benefits. Whereas the first two treaties had set aside reserves of sixty-five hectares for each family of five, the North West Angle Treaty based the allotment on one square mile (259 ha) for each family of five. Treaty Three also increased the initial payments, upped the annual payments to chiefs and head men, introduced annual grants of money for twine and ammunition, and provided for a more inclusive list of farming supplies such as implements, carpentry tools, seed, and cattle. Naturally, given the communications system among Native groups, knowledge of these advances quickly spread west and north. The result was that subsequent treaties, including the Qu'Appelle Treaty of

FIGURE 10

Treaty Six talks at Fort Carlton, 1876.

1874, incorporated the newly won gains on reserve size, payments, and equipment.

In many ways, the agreement that Big Bear would eventually sign, Treaty Six, proved the culmination of this process of bargaining, just as it revealed the thinking of Plains negotiators in the middle of the 1870s. The Cree chiefs who gathered at Fort Carlton, and later at Fort Pitt, in the summer of 1876 to negotiate with Canadian treaty commissioner Alexander Morris managed without great difficulty to obtain all the items that their brothers at Qu'Appelle, North West Angle, and Stone Fort had. In addition, they were able to push the government to greater concessions in two areas that revealed the increasing anxiety that Plains peoples felt about the basis of their way of life by 1876. Commissioner Morris spotted the evolution in Plains thinking: "The Indians," he said of the Treaty Six negotiations, "were apprehensive of their future. They saw the food supply, the buffalo, passing away, and they were anxious and distressed." That, no doubt, was why they "displayed a strong desire for instruction in farming, and appealed for the aid of missionaries and teachers." This sort of thinking caused Cree leaders to bargain for inclusion in Treaty Six of what became known as the "famine clause" and the "medicine chest" provision. The former said that, if the Cree of the Treaty Six region were "overtaken by any pestilence, or by a general famine," Canada would grant them the relief and assistance it thought appropriate. The latter said that "a medicine chest shall be kept at the house of each Indian Agent for the use and benefit of the Indians, at the discretion of such Agent."

The talks that led to Treaty Six also revealed the strategy of the Plains leaders who were prepared to enter treaty. Thanks to an account by Peter Erasmus, a mixed-blood interpreter whom the Native leaders hired, the varying positions of the chiefs have been preserved. Not all chiefs favoured making a pact with Canada. Chiefs Poundmaker, The Badger, and Young Chipewyan in particular spoke against concluding a deal in the private caucus they held between bargaining sessions with commissioner Morris. And Poundmaker publicly denounced Morris for saying that Ottawa was prepared to "give" the Cree land. "The [government] mentions how much land is to be given to us," sneered Poundmaker, a young Cree chief. "This is our land! It isn't a piece of pemmican to be cut off and given in little pieces back to us. It is ours and we will take what we want." However, in the absence of sceptics such as Big Bear, he and the other opponents of treaty were overcome by the compelling arguments of chiefs such as Mistawasis and Ahtahkakoop.

For them, treaty making was clearly part of a strategy of adjusting to threatening changes in the era of the decline of the buffalo. This was 1876 in the valley of the North Saskatchewan River, a time and place in which it was clear to all that the animals on which they had relied totally for so long were dwindling away. According to Erasmus's account, Mistawasis, who was known in English as Big Child, eloquently acknowledged "the poverty and suffering that has come to Indians because of the destruction of the buffalo as the chief source of our living, the loss of the ancient glory of our forefathers." They no longer lived in a time when "our fathers could not pass for the great number of those animals that blocked their way...." He went on to address those who opposed making treaty: "I speak directly to Poundmaker and The Badger and those others who object to signing this treaty. Have you anything better to offer our people? I ask, again, can you suggest anything that will bring these things back for tomorrow and all the tomorrows that face our people?" To him, the proposed treaty meant that "the Great White Queen Mother has offered us a way of life when the buffalo are no more. Gone they will be before many snows have come to cover our heads or graves if such should be."

To doubters, Mistawasis held out the frightening example of their Blackfoot neighbours, once bitter enemies, but now yoked with them in a community of want. From firsthand knowledge, he reported that "The Big Knives of the south came into Blackfoot territory . . ." and traded whisky first for surplus skins and then for "Blackfoot horses, buffalo robes, and all other things they had to offer." The Blackfoot were debauched, impoverished, and defeated by whisky in a manner that Cree weapons had never been able to accomplish. The demoralization of the Blackfoot had ended only recently when "The Great Queen Mother, hearing of the sorrows of her children, sent out the Red Coats." The mounted police had run the liquor traders out of the country, destroyed whisky posts such as Whoop-Up and Slide-Out, and restored peace — all with a very small force. And why, Mistawasis asked his fellow chiefs gathered in caucus near Fort Carlton, were the Mounties able to accomplish this? "Let me tell you why these things were so. It was the power that stands behind those few Red Coats that those men feared and wasted no time in getting out when they could; the power that is represented in all the Queen's people, and we the children are counted as important as even the Governor who is her personal speaker." The disappearing buffalo and whisky were the problems; the queen's maternal concern and red-coated authority were the solutions.

Mistawasis's fellow chief, Ahtahkakoop (Star Blanket), supported his argument and drew the assembly to what the two leaders thought the inevitable conclusion. "We are weak," said Ahtahkakoop, "and my brother Mista-wa-sis I think is right that the buffalo will be gone forever before many snows. What then will be left us with which to bargain? With the buffalo gone we will have only the vacant prairie which none of us have learned to use." They had to decide between resistance and agreement. "Can we stop the power of the white man from spreading over the land like the grasshoppers that cloud the sky and then fall to consume every blade of grass and every leaf on the trees in their path? I think not. Before this happens let us ponder carefully our choice of roads." The traditional path offered no hope to the Cree. "We have always lived and received our needs in clothing, shelter, and food from the countless multitudes of buffalo that have been with us since the earliest memory of our people," but that way of life was disappearing. "No-one with open eyes and open minds can doubt that the buffalo will soon be a thing of the past," lamented Ahtahkakoop. "Will our people live as

FIGURE II

Treaty medal.

before when this comes to pass? No! They will die and become just a memory unless we find another way," he warned.

Like Mistawasis, Chief Ahtahkakoop found "another way" in their two mothers, one ancient and traditional, the other new and promising. "The mother earth has always given us plenty with the grass that fed the buffalo. Surely we Indians can learn the ways of living that made the white man strong and able to vanquish all the great tribes of the southern nations." They could — they must — learn from the white man, who was coming into their country whether the Cree liked it or not. "The white men never had the buffalo but I am told they have cattle in the thousands that are covering the prairie for miles and will replace the buffalo in the Long Knives' country and may even spread over our lands." They could get their livelihood from mother earth in a new way, as the white people did, but they would need help to learn how and protection against disasters as they learned. This was where Canada, or "the White Queen Mother," came in: it could provide the necessary instruction, assistance, and protection. Ahtahkakoop argued that there was only one viable path before them. "I will accept the Queen's hand for my people," he told the chiefs in caucus. "I have spoken."

Based on such reasoning, Mistawasis, Ahtahkakoop, and other Cree leaders, some of them reluctantly, put their marks on the document that Alexander Morris had prepared. From Canada's point of view, the central feature of Treaty Six was that the Cree people surrendered control of about 310,800 square kilometres covering present-day central Saskatchewan and Alberta. Moreover, they agreed to live in peace and harmony with the queen's subjects and laws. From the standpoint of the Cree, one of the most important features of the agreement was the statement in an introductory clause that one of the purposes of the treaty was to make arrangements about the land "so that there may be peace and good will between" the Natives and the government.

The treaty also said that the Cree could continue "to pursue their avocations of hunting and fishing throughout the tract

FIGURE 12

Blackfoot chief wearing medal and triennial suit.

surrendered" until Canada required it "for settlement, mining, lumbering or other purposes." To support this maintenance of part of the traditional economy, Canada would provide $1,500 each year for "the purchase of ammunition and twine for nets for the use of the said Indians." The bands assembled at Fort Carlton would receive "reserves for farming lands" of 259 hectares per family of five, farming equipment and stock, one thousand dollars collectively if they took up their reserves by 1879, and "schools for instruction in such reserves." And, finally, there were significant financial and other material inducements. Each member of a band would receive an initial payment of twelve dollars and a yearly payment of five dollars; the chiefs and head men would receive additional annual payments of twenty-five dollars and fifteen dollars respectively. Every three years they would receive "a suitable suit of clothing, and each Chief shall receive, in recognition of the closing of the treaty, a suitable flag and medal, and also, as soon as convenient, one horse, harness and waggon."

Treaty Six represented the strategy for adjustment about which Mistawasis and Ahtahkakoop had spoken so eloquently in the caucus outside Fort Carlton. Recognizing both that the foundation of their economy, the buffalo, was vanishing and that pale-skinned newcomers were irresistibly coming into the country, they chose to establish an agreement governing their future relationship with Canada and the land. Making treaty was a means for obtaining the materials and instruction necessary to make the transition from a migratory economy based on buffalo, forest game, and fish to one dependent on growing crops and raising cattle. Because treaty making was the core of a strategy of economic adjustment, it was the Native negotiators who insisted all along on the inclusion of such provisions as agricultural instruction, schools on reserves, implements, and livestock. The government of Canada only wanted to provide initial payments, annuities, and reserves, but Saulteaux, Cree, and Blackfoot leaders proved more farsighted. Their strategic thinking came out most clearly in the negotiations at Fort Carlton in 1876, which added the "famine clause" and the "medicine chest" provision to the list of concessions that previous negotiators had extracted at Fort Qu'Appelle, North West Angle, and Stone Fort. Mistawasis, Ahtahkakoop, and other Cree leaders concluded Treaty Six in 1876 because they saw an agreement with the Dominion of Canada as the best of a series of uncongenial choices for their future. Ahtahkakoop put the point plainly: as the buffalo disappeared, he decided that "I will accept the Queen's hand for my people."

SAVE ME FROM WHAT I MOST DREAD

Big Bear was sceptical about this strategy. He was not the only Cree leader who opposed the approach of Mistawasis and Ahtahkakoop, but he would soon emerge as the main opponent of treaty making. Big Bear and his followers were still heavily dependent on hunting, unlike some other groups who had been experimenting with agriculture. Moreover, unlike Sweet Grass, the senior chief with whom Big Bear was still allied, Mistahimusqua had not been converted to Christianity. He still followed the ancient ways of acknowledging the Creator, the sun, and the multitude of spirits that animated and governed all creation. Accordingly, he was less susceptible to the influence of the missionaries who spoke in favour of making treaty. Sweet Grass, who would be murdered shortly after he agreed to treaty in September 1876, apparently was satisfied to follow the course of action that Mistawasis and Ahtahkakoop had sponsored at Fort Carlton. He told Peter Erasmus, the interpreter at Fort Carlton, that if those respected chiefs had signed the treaty, then he would do the same. Big Bear was not hostile to dealing with the white men, but he had had a different kind of experience with them. His contacts had been not with priests or pastors but with the Hudson's Bay Company traders at Fort Carlton and Fort Pitt. While he did not necessarily pick up hostility to Canada from them, neither was he likely to hear a lot of praise from them about the reliability of the government in Ottawa. Nor did he hear support for depending strictly on agriculture from men who were themselves still engaged in trade and who wanted him and his followers to keep supplying buffalo skins, now usually to Factor McKay at Fort Pitt. There was little in Big Bear's geographic, religious, or economic experience that inclined him to turn his back on the traditional Plains way of life in favour of the path that Mistawasis and Ahtahkakoop had selected.

In any event, these concerns only became significant for Big Bear after treaty documents had been signed both at Fort Carlton in August and at Fort Pitt the next month. Of course, none of the Cree bands oriented toward the post at Fort Pitt or the Christian missions farther up the North Saskatchewan had been at the parleys at Fort Carlton. And when Alexander Morris and the government treaty party moved on from Carlton to Pitt in an effort to conclude a similar agreement there, the timing was inconvenient for bands still out on the plains. The early autumn was the ideal time for hunting the buffalo cow, the preferred gender, for its flesh was heaviest at that season. Moreover, the end of summer served to remind these bands of the pressing necessity to lay in and preserve large stocks of foodstuffs for the long winter ahead. Commissioner Morris, when told that the Fort Pitt bands would be away hunting, sent messengers in search of Sweet Grass to request his presence at Fort Pitt before the government party left Carlton. Sweet Grass and his sixty-seven lodges came in to Fort Pitt on 7 September, two days after Morris had arrived there.

The talks at Fort Pitt hardly deserved the term negotiations. Sweet Grass and the other leaders of the Cree and Saulteaux bands seemed content to sign on terms similar to those agreed upon the previous month. Sweet Grass echoed Mistawasis and Ahtahkakoop in talking of the likely disappearance of the buffalo and the necessity of learning how to cultivate the land. If there were any doubters among the leaders assembled at Fort Pitt, reassurance about making treaty with Canada came from both the Catholic and Methodist missionaries in attendance.

More significantly, perhaps, Big Bear and his large following were still out hunting while the talks went on briefly at Fort Pitt. In any event a number of chiefs followed the lead of Sweet Grass and agreed to the terms that Morris offered on 9 September 1876. When Big Bear had his chance to speak to Morris four days later, his tone was very different from that of his mentor. He explained, first, that he felt inhibited in speaking because a number of bands were still out hunting. "I have come off," he told Morris, "to speak for the different bands that are out on the plains. It is no small matter we were to consult about. I expected the Chiefs here would have waited until I arrived." Although the bands still out hunting had told Big Bear that he should "speak in their stead," he was reluctant to do so now that treaty had been made. "The people who have not come, stand as a barrier before what I would have had to say; my mode of living is hard," Morris reported him as explaining. Perhaps partly in embarrassment over acting without Big Bear, Sweet Grass urged his younger colleague to speak to "the representative of the Queen here" and to make treaty, too. ". . . I feel," continued Sweet Grass, "as if I saw life when I see the representative of the Queen; let nothing be a barrier between you and him; it is through great difficulty this has been brought to us. Think of our children and those to come after, there is life and succor for them; say yes and take his hand."

As he stared at Sweet Grass and Morris, Big Bear was in a dilemma. Treaty had been made, and the elder chief was urging him to join in, but he had a mandate only to represent the other hunting bands in negotiations, not to accept a previously fashioned document. Moreover, he did not know Morris as well as Sweet Grass and some others seemed to know him. He knew the Bay's man, W.J. Christie, who was with Morris, but he did not know the queen's spokesman. Under pressure, Big Bear uttered words whose misconstruction would haunt him: "Stop, stop, my friends, I have never seen the Governor [Morris] before; I have seen Mr. Christie many times. I heard the Governor was to come and I said I shall see him; when I see him I will make a request that he will save me from what I most dread, that is: the rope to be about my neck. . . ." The translator told Morris that Big Bear had said that he was reluctant to make treaty, not literally because he feared "the rope to be about my neck" but, as Morris inserted the word in his account, because he feared "hanging." Morris stiffened and replied that "No good Indian has the rope about his neck." The misunderstanding about hanging continued, and the talks between Morris and Big Bear ended without any agreement or even clarification of the points that the Cree chief had hoped to negotiate.

This fateful misunderstanding was both a revelation of the cultural abyss that separated Cree and Canadian negotiators and a foreshadowing of where misunderstanding would draw both Cree and Canada over the next decade. When he spoke to Morris, Big Bear, like Native spokesmen generally, employed a highly metaphorical style of rhetoric that coloured and enlivened his language. As John Tobias has explained in "The Origins of the Treaty Rights Movement in Saskatchewan," it was typical of Big Bear and others to use terms meaningful within their own cultural settings. For example, Cree negotiators used homely terms of family and kinship to describe themselves and their anticipated relationship to the queen and her government. Such usage was in keeping with Native diplomacy generally. In Aboriginal societies, kinship of one form or another was required in order to conduct economic or political business, because the ties that counted were those of kin. So, where genuine kinship did not exist, parties that wished to deal with each other created "fictive kinship," which made it possible for them to trade or conclude a pact of peace or mutual assistance. That cultural requirement explains why talks between Native chieftains and European military leaders were usually studded with references to "our brothers," "our cousins," or "the great white father" or "mother."

However, when Native leaders on the prairies in the 1870s referred to themselves as "children" and asked the "queen mother" to "pity" them, they did so against a background in which children occupied a privileged position. In Plains culture, childhood was a time of great individual autonomy and self-indulgence, a brief period when the young experienced very little direct restraint from adults in the community. Childhood, to the Cree, was a time of freedom and delight, during which the young enjoyed a right to be provided for and assisted by the adults. In contrast, among Euro-Canadians, whose child-rearing techniques were dramatically different from those of these Aboriginal groups, childhood was a time of dependence and submission. Children in non-Native society were expected to be "seen but not heard," to be obedient and well behaved, and not to impose on their parents or other adults. Given these contrasting cultural views of childhood, Plains and government negotiators meant to convey quite different messages even when they used the same words. Cree references to themselves as "children" and to Queen Victoria as their "mother" implied the autonomy that they wished to enjoy in relationship with her government, from which they expected help when needed. However, government negotiators such as Alexander Morris got a very different message from such talk. In marked contrast to Saulteaux and Cree leaders, when he spoke the language of a parent-child relationship during negotiations, he invariably tied it to notions of obedience and good behaviour.

This sort of misunderstanding unfortunately occurred during the conversation between Big Bear and Morris at Fort Pitt in September 1876. The Cree chief was speaking metaphorically when he referred to a fear of "the rope to be about my neck." Coming as he did from a Plains society in which the horse was central to his people's way of life, he obviously had in mind himself as a horse and the rope as a bridle. His reference thus expressed his aversion to the loss of freedom for him and his people that might ensue from making treaty. Big Bear was telling the treaty commissioner metaphorically that he was not willing to make treaty if it meant submission to Canadian law and control. Morris, understandably given the inadequate translation of Big Bear's speech, misunderstood the Cree leader to be saying that he was afraid of being hanged. The puzzled commissioner told Big Bear that "No good Indian has the rope about his neck," and, when the chief continued to voice his concern, asked bluntly, "why are you so anxious about bad men?" The misunderstanding created the impression that Big Bear was a potential troublemaker who would have to be watched carefully. After all, if he did not harbour some evil intent, why did he fear the rope?

For the moment, Big Bear and Morris had to leave their discussion in an inconclusive state. Before they parted, the chief tried to explain his reluctance to come to a conclusion and to underline his positive disposition toward Morris's mission. For example, he tried again to express his people's concern that the treaty promise action to conserve the buffalo when he gestured to his fellow leaders at Fort Pitt and said, "Then these Chiefs will help us to protect the buffalo, that there may be enough for all." He also repeated that he felt he had to consult "his people before he acted." His final words to Morris at the public discussions were: "I am glad to meet you, I am alone; but if I had known the time, I would have been here with all my people. I am not an undutiful child, I do not throw back your hand; but as my people are not here, I do not sign. I will tell them what I have heard, and next year I will come." Privately, according to Morris, Big Bear told Canada's negotiator that he was favourably disposed toward making treaty and would return the following year "to meet the Commissioners and accept it." By now, however, Morris harboured serious doubts about Big Bear. Those doubts would serve as a foundation on which government officials would build a virulent hostility toward chiefs who did not fall in easily with Ottawa's plans. For example, Hayter Reed, a future deputy minister of Indian Affairs, would refer to chiefs such as Big Bear and Little Pine who opposed making treaty as "the scum of the Plains."

Events in the few years after the 1876 meeting at Fort Pitt served to confirm Big Bear's reluctance to make treaty while enhancing his prestige and influence among the Plains groups around the North Saskatchewan valley. The death of Sweet

Grass a short time after the conclusion of Treaty Six weakened the influence of the Christianized pro-treaty leaders. Inevitably, Big Bear, now in his early fifties and at the height of his diplomatic and political powers, emerged as the dominant chief of the bands along the northern branch of the river. The number of his followers continued to swell as opponents of treaty making gravitated toward his camp; by 1878 or 1879, he was the leader of approximately two thousand men, women, and children. He was as good as his word to Alexander Morris, returning to Fort Pitt for further discussions in 1877, but the fact that Ottawa had sent a minor official who had no authority to vary the conditions for treaty ensured that no agreement was reached. The increasingly influential Mistahimusqua grew firmer in his opposition to making treaty on the basis the other chiefs had in 1876.

What strengthened his opposition was his knowledge that many chiefs who had entered treaty soon regretted their decision. During the late 1870s and early 1880s, the government of Canada proved extremely slow to implement many of the provisions of the agreements, leading some to speculate cynically that Ottawa was losing interest in its obligations now that treaties had been concluded for the entire prairie region. It was several years before surveyors came to some districts covered by Treaty Six to lay out the reserves that had been promised, and often it took longer for implements and livestock to be supplied to them. When farming instructors eventually made their way to Indian communities along the North Saskatchewan, they often turned out to be political appointees who had no training in teaching agriculture, particularly the techniques of farming that would be necessary for success on the harsh prairies and parklands. By 1879, Regina newspaper publisher Nicholas Flood Davin was remarking that chiefs such as Beardy, whose reserve was near Duck Lake, and Big Bear were "malcontent."

In fact, Big Bear's doubts about the treaties were being reinforced, not just by the government's tardy and inadequate follow-up, but also by the advice of family and fellow chiefs. In particular, his older sons Twin Wolverine and Imasees, the latter also known sometimes as Little Bear, were strongly opposed to having anything to do with the white men and their ways. And at least one other significant chief, Little Pine, remained out of treaty in the years after 1876. These various influences tended to strengthen Big Bear's doubts. Finally, in 1878, he came to a conclusion that he communicated to Canada's lieutenant-governor for the Northwest Territories, David Laird. According to a version published five years later as "Big Bear Rises to Explain" in the *Saskatchewan Herald*, a weekly newspaper printed in Battleford, Big Bear told Laird that he would wait and watch; if the government lived up to its promises in the treaties, in four years' time he would sign.

Big Bear's stance on the treaties did nothing to endear him to either the government or the citizens of Canada in these years. Officialdom in the west, increasingly concerned about opposition from the likes of Little Pine and restiveness from chiefs such as Piapot in Treaty Four, looked with anxiety on the determined opposition of Big Bear and his immense following. There was an inclination to interpret all his actions and words negatively, a tendency perhaps established by the rope-around-the-neck exchange at Fort Pitt. For the slowly growing settler population along the North Saskatchewan, holdouts such as Big Bear were a cause for worry, sometimes exaggerated worry. Given the disproportion between their small settlement of a couple of hundred and Big Bear's camp of two thousand, the citizens of the Battleford area might have been forgiven for their "great amount of unnecessary nervousness," on which Indian Commissioner Edgar Dewdney commented in his annual report for 1879. It was not that Dewdney, now Ottawa's most influential man on Indian affairs in the Territories, had any higher opinion or better understanding of Big Bear than did the newspaper editor and citizens of Battleford. He, like non-Natives in general, mistook Big Bear's watchful stance for a threatening attitude. Big Bear, the "malcontent" as Davin described him, continued to be dogged by the faulty perception of him that had originated in his tangled talks with Morris in 1876.

During his four-year wait after 1878, Big Bear had little time to worry about what the likes of Davin or Dewdney thought about him, because there were far more pressing concerns to occupy him. The major preoccupation was the increasing scarcity of buffalo, on which his group continued to rely overwhelmingly. Each year, it seemed, the herds became harder to locate and harvest. Some Plains people believed that they had offended the spirit of the buffalo, or that an evil spirit had hidden the herds away from them in a vast cave as punishment for some violation of required behaviour. A few traditionalists thought that their offence had been to make treaties with Canada between 1871 and 1877. Non-Natives attributed the scarcity, which they also increasingly recognized as a problem in the late 1870s, to overhunting by both Aboriginal peoples and non-Natives alike. Decades of strong demand for hides were coming to a frightening, climactic conclusion.

For Big Bear, a major responsibility was to help his people find whatever herds still existed or were not being hidden from them by a malign spirit. Between 1878 and 1882, he found it necessary to lead his huge following through much of the prairie region, often deserting the North Saskatchewan valley for long periods. Sometimes they congregated with other suffering groups near the Cypress Hills, but their presence there unnerved the North West Mounted Police. The policemen were always anxious about large numbers of hunters and warriors congregating anywhere, but they were particularly frightened between 1876 and 1881 because the Cypress Hills were the home base for thousands of refugee Sioux under Sitting Bull, the leader of the forces that had defeated General Custer and the American Seventh Cavalry at the Battle of the Little Big Horn. Whenever leaders such as Big Bear, Piapot, or others turned up at Fort Walsh in these years in search of buffalo or government aid, the Mounties feared that the hardship would lead to troubles that could spark a general Indian uprising. And even when they persuaded a reluctant Sitting Bull to return to the United States, the problems did not lessen significantly. By that time, the want that all Plains hunters were facing had become acute.

To combat that hardship, Big Bear also took his followers south of the international boundary, an invisible line that had little political significance for them in any event. These forays, which never seemed to produce much success in hunting, did bring Big Bear into contact with other leaders of importance. In 1879, on the Milk River in Montana, he met and discussed Canadian concerns with Louis Riel, the Métis chieftain who had led resistance to the imposition of Canadian authority in Red River a decade earlier. Big Bear was not especially well disposed to the Red River Métis, because he and his followers had had an angry brush a number of years earlier with Gabriel Dumont and some buffalo hunters in the South Saskatchewan region, where many refugees from Red River had moved after the troubles of 1869–70. Big Bear listened without much interest to Riel's grand talk of fashioning an alliance of Métis and Plains groups to obtain justice for Aboriginal peoples in Canada. Big Bear was still pursuing his twofold strategy of waiting for Canada to live up to the treaties and trying to procure enhanced provisions for his own people before signing. He was disappointed but not dissuaded by Little Pine's decision in 1879 to enter treaty.

Big Bear also had brushes with American law that would eventually force him to return permanently to Canadian territory north of what his people called "the medicine line." In 1881, his camp encountered an American cavalry force that threatened them and ultimately drove them back across the border. According to Dempsey in *Big Bear*, later the same year, Big Bear maintained, an American official approached him and offered to create a reservation for his followers in Montana. Big Bear rejected the offer, much to the annoyance of Imasees and Twin Wolverine, who wanted them all to leave Canada permanently. This difference of strategy served to widen a growing rift between the chief — who, at fifty-six, was seen by some young rivals as ripe to be replaced — and younger men who favoured a more aggressive policy. Big Bear also knew that his strategy was opposed by Wandering Spirit, the band's war chief, who assumed leadership at times of crisis. Just such a condition developed in

FIGURE 13

Big Bear's camp near Maple Creek, 1883.

FIGURE 14

Watering horses at Big Bear's camp, 1883.

the spring of 1882, when an American military force gathered to attack Big Bear's camp in an effort to destroy it or drive its inhabitants out of American territory permanently. Thanks to Wandering Spirit's skill and decisive action, the community was able to elude the military, but this threat convinced Big Bear he had to leave the land of the Long Knives for good. In the spring of 1882, once again in the leadership now that the war emergency had passed, he took his followers across the line to Fort Walsh in the Cypress Hills district. It was perhaps ominous that Indian Commissioner Dewdney, in his report for 1881, had referred to Canadian Natives in American territory as "the most worthless and troublesome Indians we have."

Dr. Augustus Jukes had a much more sympathetic evaluation when he encountered Big Bear's followers fewer than six months after their return to Canada. In a letter now held in the Department of Indian Affairs records, the North West Mounted Police surgeon reported that the two thousand camped near Fort Walsh in the autumn of 1882 were "literally in a starving condition and destitute of the commonest necessaries of life." He had seen "little children at this inclement season, snow having already fallen, who had scarcely rags to cover them. Of food they possessed little or none. . . ." Not just their clothing was inadequate and in short supply, he noted. They also lacked lodges "to shield them from the inclemency of the impending winter. Few of their lodges are of Buffalo hide, the majority being of cotton only, many of these in the most rotten and dilapidated condition." The reason for this destitution? As Dr. Jukes correctly noted, their poverty and hardship stemmed from the "disappearance of the Buffalo."

Chief Big Bear and his people were in extreme peril of starving. Over the previous four years, they had extended the normal range of their hunt for the buffalo to include large areas south of the international boundary. Their ranging had brought them a drastically decreasing harvest of buffalo meat and an increasing exposure to hostile American forces. Through the worsening of their conditions, the anger and opposition of younger men such as his own sons and war chief Wandering Spirit had risen, and some of the families had quietly left his camp and attached themselves to other chiefs who were in treaty and receiving payments and food assistance for their followers. Even though all the reports that Big Bear received while in the United States and after he returned to the Cypress Hills area in the spring of 1882 convinced him that the government of Canada was not living up to its treaty commitments, he had to abandon his policy of staying out of treaty. A chief's fundamental obligation was to look after his people according to his best judgement of their interests. In the past, Big Bear had interpreted this obligation as necessitating a rejection of treaty; however, by the autumn of 1882, the spectre of starvation forced him to reverse his decision.

Ever true to his reputation as a tough fighter for the interests of his followers, Big Bear did not capitulate easily to the treaty makers at Fort Walsh in 1882. (They, for their part, continued to believe wrongly that the reason he had spurned treaty was, in the words of Allan McDonald, the Indian agent at Fort Walsh, "his great objection to hanging, as punishment for murder.") In preliminary discussions with the agent, Big Bear insisted that "he wanted some more money than had been promised in the Treaty" before he would sign, but Indian Affairs and NWMP officials told him that such a concession was out of the question. Even when the old chief met with the agent to sign his adherence to Treaty Six, he launched into a speech about his people's needs that lasted for four hours until he was interrupted. Significantly, it was "his son and son-in-law" who stopped him and urged the reluctant Big Bear to put his mark on two copies of the treaty. The buffalo gone, his policy of watching and waiting having run its course, his followers starving and in some cases abandoning him, and under severe pressure from younger members of his following, the last holdout among the northern Plains leaders entered treaty on 8 December 1882.

CREE DIPLOMAT

Although Big Bear had been forced by hunger to enter treaty, he did not propose to settle down quietly to a life of submission. Still opposed to having the rope of Canadian law around his neck, he would manoeuvre over the next few years to maximize the autonomy that the Plains people still possessed. In part, his post-1882 strategy emphasized concentrating Indians in particular regions of the North West Territories in order to retain a compact territory separate from the changes that agricultural settlers would bring, as well as to make the chiefs' influence as great as possible by assembling a large body of people in a single locality. The second part of his policy was an effort to unite Plains, more particularly Cree, leadership for the purpose of applying political pressure on the government of Canada to revise the treaties in favour of the prairie peoples. The background to all of this, however, was the continuing problems of no buffalo and opposition from the American military to allowing any Indians from Canada to stay in American territory for any lengthy period. Caught between the obstinacy of Canada and the hostility of the United States, Big Bear would struggle from 1883 onward to advance his people's cause by diplomatic means in an arena in which the choices available to him and his followers were steadily diminishing.

The chief attempted to counter — without much success — the negative image of him and his intentions that had developed in the small settler communities in the Territories. He tried valiantly to reassure western settlers that he was not a troublemaker and that he had had sound reasons for the things he had done in the years after 1876. In the summer of 1882, for example, he took the extraordinary step of sending a message to the editor of the *Saskatchewan Herald* to correct inaccurate and inflammatory reports about him. In "Big Bear Rises to Explain," he pointed out to readers on 5 August 1882 that his earlier refusal to enter treaty was "not due to any feeling of ill-will to the Government, but solely because of a vow that he would watch for a certain length of time to see whether the Government would faithfully carry out its promises to the Indians." During the wait-and-see period, he continued, far from being a source of trouble, he had always sought to deter troublemakers. So, he contended, he had dismissed the advice from Louis Riel and Indian leaders based in American territory to organize for a struggle against Canada. As further proof of his pacific nature, he also told the *Saskatchewan Herald* about the time that he had corrected a young follower by seizing a horse from him and returning it to its rightful owner, only to be beaten with a stick by the young man. On that occasion, Big Bear said, he had not retaliated against the angry young man. So far as he could, Big Bear tried in the early 1880s to reassure settlers and government that his course continued to be a peaceful one.

If the editor of the *Saskatchewan Herald* was any gauge of settler opinion, Big Bear might just as well have saved his words, for the chief continued to be an object of suspicion and hostility. The Battleford newspaper, for example, remained inclined to expect the worst and exaggerate the reality of Indian actions. The only variation in this treatment was an occasional lapse into ridicule of leaders such as Big Bear. On 4 August 1883, for example, the paper regaled its readers with an account of a supposed encounter between Big Bear and a travelling photographer. When the photographer had asked him to pose for a picture, the chief allegedly had replied that he "was a great man, whose name was known everywhere, and the desire for his photograph was so wide-spread that its sale would bring a fortune to the man who could secure it, and that therefore it must be paid for." According to this account, the photographer declined to pay Big Bear's price, and no photograph was taken at Battleford. A more likely interpretation is that the chief was either having a joke at the expense of the traveller or simply did not want to be bothered by him. In any event, anything he did was misinterpreted by hostile non Native opinion makers.

It was, then, against this background of misunderstanding and hostility that Big Bear tried to adjust to his unaccustomed status as leader of hundreds of Cree in treaty. Particularly difficult from his point of view was Indian Commissioner Edgar Dewdney, who increasingly shaped the application of government policy toward Plains Indians from 1879 until the middle of the 1880s. Dewdney, a loyal follower of Conservative leader Sir John A. Macdonald, had already shown his character in interactions with Native leaders in the Cypress Hills area. In 1880, he had promised Chief Piapot and Chief Little Pine, and any Cree who wanted to, that they could have reserves in the Cypress Hills, a traditional gathering place rich in game and wood supplies. Soon, however, government officials realized that if these commitments were carried out, there was a strong possibility that the Cypress Hills would become an Indian territory controlled by Assiniboine and Cree through the sheer force of their numbers. Once Ottawa's men figured out what Piapot and other leaders had in mind, the bureaucrats reneged on treaty undertakings to allow bands to select reserves where they wished. Instead, Piapot was forced to move a considerable distance to the northeast and settle in the Qu'Appelle Valley, and plans were laid to cajole or compel bands to scatter between three localities: Qu'Appelle, the Battleford district, and the Fort Pitt region.

By the time Big Bear made treaty, the government's perfidy had become obvious. Piapot returned to the Cypress Hills area that summer to warn that, judging by the shabby way he had been treated by officials at Fort Qu'Appelle, the chiefs could not trust the government to honour its promises. In 1882, Dewdney had served notice on the various bands still congregated in the Cypress Hills that the police post at nearby Fort Walsh would be closed. This meant that a source of provisions for bands unsuccessful in the hunt would be shut down. His purpose in closing Fort Walsh, in the spring of 1883, was to force the bands to move out of the region and to disperse to the Qu'Appelle, Battleford, and Fort Pitt areas. By now, Dewdney and other government officials knew that the American military would repel any parties that made their way into American territory, and the continuing spectre of want and starvation meant that the harsh policy the police and Indian Affairs department were adopting would put unbearable pressure on Big Bear and other leaders to scatter. Sure enough, the government's strategy seemed to be working, for Piapot returned to the Qu'Appelle valley in 1883 and took a reserve near a large concentration of Assiniboine who were already there, while Little Pine and Lucky Man took up reserves near Poundmaker and his people in the Battleford area. All that remained, so far as the government officials were concerned, was to force Big Bear north to the Fort Pitt district. Not only would that get the powerful chief out of the Cypress Hills and away from the American border, but it would also complete the process of scattering the most powerful Cree leaders to different areas of the North West Territories.

As usual, Big Bear was not prepared to fall in easily with the plans that Dewdney had developed for him and his people. He would still try to avoid getting that government halter around his neck. Although he was finally persuaded to set off northward in the spring of 1883, he failed to take the path that Indian Affairs officials had in mind. They expected him to make his way directly to the Fort Pitt area, where officials had picked out a reserve for him, but he and his followers stopped in the Battleford area to consult with Poundmaker and other Indian leaders. Big Bear was disappointed, but not surprised, by Poundmaker's confirmation that Ottawa was not honouring the treaty provisions fully, especially those that had guaranteed assistance in making the transition to agriculture. Poundmaker was especially bitter because he had tried to accommodate the government's wishes that they farm, even working long and hard in the fields himself as a model for his people. However, in the years since 1876, he and other chiefs had found that the government was slow to respond to their complaints and uncooperative in providing the assistance to which they felt they were entitled. And complaints came not just from leaders in the Battleford region. Big Bear would soon learn that farther east, in the lands between the South and North Saskatchewan near Fort Carlton, chiefs such as Mistawasis and Ahtahkakoop, who had championed treaty making, were also bitter about the treatment that they had received. All of this information, coming hard on the heels of the harsh experience in the Cypress Hills, made Big Bear very dubious about following the wishes of bureaucrats. In *Big Bear*, Hugh Dempsey reports the chief as telling agent J.M. Rae at Battleford in the summer of 1883 that the Cree "are promised great things but they seem far off and we cannot live and wait."

Big Bear's reaction to his discovery that the government of Canada could not be trusted was to adopt a strategy of uniting Plains opposition to government mistreatment. One (unsuccessful) example of his policy was his request while at Battleford to take his reserve near those of Poundmaker and Little Pine, who had adjoining reserves northwest of Battleford. Had Big Bear and his five hundred followers settled in this region, they would have constituted a powerful force, because there were several Assiniboine reserves south of Battleford that augmented the numbers of Poundmaker's and Little Pine's reserves. Just as they had in the south, government officials responded negatively to this request. They feared the concentration of Indians in the Battleford region for the same reason they had in the Cypress Hills: numbers would give the Natives strength. Indian Affairs would have none of Big Bear in the Battleford district in 1883; government officials insisted that he move on to Fort Pitt.

Although Big Bear was compelled by the fear of starvation to take his band west along the North Saskatchewan to Fort Pitt, he did not abandon his general plan of organizing Native cooperation to place pressure on the government. He refused to take up the reserve that Indian Affairs officers had selected for him, choosing to remain near Fort Pitt and demanding that the mounted police commander, Inspector Francis Dickens, son of the English writer, provide supplies for them. During the winter of 1883–84, the chief, now nearing his sixtieth year, planned a diplomatic campaign to force Ottawa to treat Plains peoples fairly.

Unfortunately, government officials were taking actions of their own that would lead to a worsening of relations between

Aboriginal peoples and Canada. In response to a recession that put pressure on finances in 1883, the government ordered a series of cutbacks in most of its departments. In the case of the Department of Indian Affairs, which had been established as a separate ministry only in 1880, this decision was especially troublesome. The responsibilities of Indian Affairs, particularly in the prairie region, were increasing as the hardship following the collapse of the buffalo economy deepened. Moreover, Indian Affairs was facing the necessity of increasing its programs, in the potentially costly area of education, for example. The deputy minister of Indian Affairs made a rapid tour of the west, as Edgar Dewdney noted to the prime minister, just at harvest when reserve populations were enjoying some respite from hardship. Deputy Minister Vankoughnet rashly concluded that his department could also take its share of budget cuts and hurried back to Ottawa to implement them. Therefore, from the 1883-84 fiscal year onward, Indian Affairs officials were ordered to be even less generous with food and other forms of aid. Unfortunately, these years of the mid-1880s were characterized by severe winters, low spring and summer rainfall, and early frosts—all conditions that made farming extremely difficult in the Territories. Big Bear's followers were able to support themselves to a limited extent by casual work with the Hudson's Bay Company, by carrying freight to Fort Edmonton, for example. But such limited employment was both stopgap and inadequate. The upshot of the adverse climate, government retrenchment, and continuing hardship on the Plains was increasing unrest among the Blackfoot, Cree, and others.

At a personal level, Big Bear was also troubled by growing divisions in his immediate family. Some of his adult sons, especially Twin Wolverine and Imasees, were opposed to his strategy of pursuing diplomatic resistance rather than cooperating with Indian Affairs and settling down to life on the reserve. His oldest son, Twin Wolverine, actually left Big Bear's camp with his own family and followed another chief. Imasees, also known as Little Bear, stayed and opposed his father. In particular, Imasees had become a strong supporter of Wandering Spirit, the band's war chief, who also objected to Big Bear's program. It was not that these restless men disagreed with Big Bear's negative view of the government's behaviour. They all agreed that Ottawa, Dewdney, and the various Indian agents had not acted honourably in their dealings with the Indians. But whereas Big Bear was forever developing strategies to stave off a final showdown with officialdom — going south to hunt buffalo, remaining in the Cypress Hills till driven out by hunger, going to Battleford rather than directly to Fort Pitt, and refusing to accept the reserve selected for him — the younger group favoured more immediate and decisive action. It had been they and others of like mind who had interrupted Big Bear's four-hour harangue in December 1882 and virtually forced their chief to sign Treaty Six. As conditions worsened in the winter of 1883–84, these turbulent younger men threatened both Big Bear's hold on leadership and the peace that was necessary if his strategy of uniting the northern bands was to succeed.

In 1884, in spite of his personal worries, Big Bear set to work to combat both government and climatic problems through diplomatic means. His general strategy was to act in parallel fashion to Piapot, who was working hard in the south to unite the various bands into a cooperative force. Big Bear proposed to attempt a similar unification of the various groups in the north and to forge links with the Blackfoot far to the southwest. Instrumental in this strategy was use of the Thirst Dance, an important late-spring ceremony of the Cree people, to bring groups together and promote a spirit of unity. The Thirst Dance was similar to the Sun Dance of the Blackfoot people, a religious and social ritual that marked important passages in the life cycle and built community cohesion. The dance could be sponsored by someone who had promised to hold such an event if delivered from some peril during a time of crisis. Sometimes during the Thirst Dance, young men endured a painful ritual that involved dancing while attached to the central pole of the dance lodge by ropes leading to pinions through the skin of their chests. They danced until they collapsed from exhaustion or the flesh tore. Thirst Dances were also social and political occasions during which people overcame divisions and bound themselves more closely together. It was this latter purpose that Big Bear pursued during dances and councils in 1884, first on the Little Pine reserve near Battleford and then near Duck Lake in the Fort Carlton region.

Although the Thirst Dances and councils caused unease among government officials, they did advance at least part of Big Bear's two-point agenda. As he told Dewdney (who passed the information on to Prime Minister Macdonald), he "wanted [the Native bands] to ask for a large Reserve altogether," but he also hoped that they would authorize him to speak on their united behalf with the government of Canada. The *Saskatchewan Herald*, as usual, put his attitude on government relations unkindly on 8 March 1884, when it lampooned him. According to the newspaper, Big Bear was fed up dealing with officials in the west, none of whom seemed to be "the government" that made the decisions. "To this end he has made up his mind to go to Ottawa, calling at Regina on his way," to make the western Indians' case to the government. Without knowing how close it was to the truth, the Battleford newspaper got at a central part of Big Bear's strategy: if he could unite the bands of Treaty Six and possibly Treaty Four, where Piapot was influential, to authorize him to speak on their behalf, then his hand would be greatly strengthened as he attempted to get the government to improve conditions. Although the *Saskatchewan Herald* understood it but dimly — and, of course, attempted to paint it in a ridiculous light — there was a clear plan behind Big Bear's arranging for Thirst Dances to be held.

His strategy was only partially successful in 1884. In spite of the opposition of Edgar Dewdney and the Indian department, the chief and many of his followers managed to make their way to the Little Pine reserve without being stopped by the police. Moreover, once the dance rituals were held and discussions took place, the old chief did manage to persuade the other leaders that he should speak on behalf of all of them in future dealings with the government. This was a considerable accomplishment, for it meant that Big Bear would be able to claim a sizeable Plains following if Piapot succeeded in uniting the southern groups behind the strategy. On the negative side of the Battleford experience was the fact that Commissioner Dewdney, with whom Big Bear met, informed him and other leaders that the department would not permit Big Bear's band and several others to take up reserves in proximity to Poundmaker and Little Pine. Officialdom understood their object in seeking reserves together, and it intended to frustrate the plan.

A more serious setback, one retrieved from complete disaster fortunately, was an altercation between young warriors and an Indian Affairs employee during the Thirst Dance at Little Pine reserve. Farm instructor John Craig abruptly refused to issue food to a number of young men, leading one of them to strike him on the arm with an axe handle. When the mounted police came to the reserve the next day to arrest the men who had had the confrontation with Craig, they walked into a very tense situation. Their unwitting intrusion into the Thirst Dance lodge, considered sacred by the Cree, angered the young men and almost resulted in bloodshed when gunfire broke out. Another farm instructor who was present, Robert Jefferson, later recalled that when some of the warriors began firing their rifles, they were "merely trying to frighten us, as the bullets that whistled over our heads might just as easily have been sent into our midst." Jefferson was right: the warriors were prepared to wipe out the officials and police were the latter to fire at them, but they would not be the first to shoot *at* someone. Luckily, no one fired at anybody, and eventually the police were able to arrest and remove the two men they sought for the assault on Craig. The tense affair aroused ill feeling and evoked once again the image of Big Bear as a "bad Indian" who — for good reason — feared a rope around his neck.

Events following the Battleford Thirst Dance intensified the settlers' negative view of Big Bear. When the chief and his followers were on their way back to Fort Pitt after the dance, they were overtaken by messengers from an unexpected source. As NWMP Superintendent Crozier informed the police commissioner, "the emissaries of Riel" — for that was who the messengers were — "invited [Big Bear] to meet that person at Duck Lake." The mysterious Métis leader had come to the South Saskatchewan Métis communities in June, invited by Gabriel Dumont and other leading men to provide leadership for their campaign to get the government to redress their grievances over land issues. Big Bear took advantage of this unexpected invitation. At Duck Lake, he participated in a large council of Cree leaders at which venerable chiefs such as Mistawasis and Ahtahkakoop, who had been energetic in promoting the making of treaty, were loud in their denunciation of the government's failure to live up to its commitments. Big Bear was also able to have a meeting with Riel, but he made no commitments to the Métis leader about any future action. Although invited back to the South Saskatchewan to lead a peaceful protest, the Métis leader seemed to be trying to fashion a united front of Métis and Indians against the government. However Riel's strategy was developing, Big Bear remained dedicated to his plan of uniting all the Cree leaders, and if possible the Blackfoot, to press for a renegotiation of the treaties that would provide more assistance to the hard-pressed Plains people.

As was by now becoming depressingly familiar, Big Bear's journey to the Fort Carlton area was misinterpreted by officials and newspapers. Uninformed observers claimed that the Duck Lake council had been Big Bear's idea all along, when in fact it had been called by the local leadership. What alarmed government officials was that men such as Mistawasis and Ahtahkakoop, whom Ottawa had always regarded as cooperative, were now apparently joining with someone whom officials regarded as an opponent of their policies. The reaction from Dewdney's quarter was to urge a more forceful policy for dealing with leaders such as Big Bear. What was needed, wrote Dewdney, was "sheer compulsion." Over the winter of 1884–85, the Indian Act was amended to authorize officials to arrest any Indian who was on another band's reserve without the approval of the local Indian Affairs officials. The government also considered amending the act to require anyone who left a reserve to get a pass signed by the agent, but were advised that such a requirement would violate treaty guarantees of freedom of movement. But the changes to the Indian Act, and the decision to increase the number of police in Cree country for 1885, indicated that Ottawa, as usual, was interpreting the actions of Big Bear and others, especially now that Riel was back in the country, as warnings of trouble.

Over the winter of 1884–85, Big Bear remained in the Fort Pitt area making plans for the continuation of his diplomatic strategy in the spring. It had not proven possible in the summer of 1884 to make his trip to see "the government" on behalf of the bands of Treaty Six, but considerable progress had been made in uniting the Cree. In 1885, he foresaw, he and other like-minded chiefs would continue with their political offensive, trying yet again to get the Blackfoot Confederacy to join with them to unite all the major Plains nations in a solid phalanx. Riel's activity at the head of a Métis movement of protest, though cooperation with Riel and Dumont was not part of Big Bear's plans, was also potentially helpful because it made the government anxious about unrest in the west. Big Bear probably realized that he was being carefully watched that winter by the policeman in charge of Fort Pitt, Francis Dickens. Dickens, for example, reported that Little Poplar had come into the Fort Pitt district and would probably winter with Big Bear's people, recounted Big Bear's angry speech about the treatment he had received at a council at Fort Pitt in October, and carefully counted the lodges of Big Bear's band, which now numbered about five hundred. While Mistahimusqua planned, various officials watched and prepared countermoves.

What none of the players in the northwestern drama could control in 1884 and 1885 were the severe climatic conditions, which continued to cause hardship for all the inhabitants, but especially for the Natives. The harvest in 1884 had been poor, and the winter of 1884-85 was extremely harsh, with bitterly low temperatures and heavy snowfalls. Big Bear's continuing refusal to select a reserve meant that the policy Indian Affairs had been following since at least 1883 of refusing rations to bands that refused to settle on reserves was applied to his people. To the intense anger of his opponents, Big Bear and his drawn-out strategy were causing great hardship. The band was able to reduce its suffering somewhat by cutting firewood for the Department of Indian Affairs, but severe weather limited this means of getting hold of cash to buy provisions. Hunkered down in their winter encampment near Frog Lake — a settlement that had a Hudson's Bay Company storehouse, an Indian agency, and a Roman Catholic mission in addition to a small population of non-Native farmers — Big Bear was at last forced to concede. Under pressure from Imasees and some of the other young men, he agreed to select his reserve at a point about halfway between Frog Lake and Saddle Lake in the spring. They had made it very clear that if their chief did not take a reserve in 1885, many of them would leave him and join other bands. Ironically, as his broad diplomatic strategy seemed on the verge of success, Big Bear had to acknowledge that he was severely weakened as the leader of his own people. His role as chief hung by a thread.

"THE TROUBLE-MAKERS WERE BEYOND MY CONTROL"

Late in March 1885, Mistahimusqua was on his way back to the encampment near Frog Lake when trouble broke out in the Saskatchewan country. News arrived of an armed encounter between Métis horsemen and mounted police at Duck Lake that had resulted in the deaths of nine civilians and three Mounties. The news excited many of the younger men, who were inclined to listen to Wandering Spirit, the war chief, and Imasees. By the time the old chief returned from hunting, the warriors were effectively in charge of the community, and his influence as civil

FIGURE 15

Theresa Gowanlock, prisoner of Wandering Spirit, 1885.

chief was no longer in effect. Wandering Spirit especially seemed determined to push for aggressive action against the non-Native population. The final factor bringing on disaster at Frog Lake was the alcohol that some of the young men obtained after looting a storehouse. Among the trophies of their raid was some liquid painkiller, a popular concoction that contained a high proportion of alcohol. Armed men who drank the painkiller became increasingly turbulent.

The final outbreak at Frog Lake occurred on the morning of 2 April, almost a week after the clash between police and Métis at Duck Lake. Unknown to Big Bear, Wandering Spirit and a party of armed warriors went to the settlement and rounded up all the non-Natives. They also began raiding the Hudson's Bay Company stores, but quit when Big Bear, who arrived in the midst of these activities, urged them not to take anything without permission. Trouble continued to build, thanks in no small part to the influence of alcohol. When Indian agent Thomas Quinn, having consulted Big Bear, refused to obey Wandering Spirit's instructions that all the prisoners leave the official settlement and go to the Indian camp, he was shot dead by the war chief. This action sparked a general attack on the prisoners, many of whom had already set off on the trail toward the camp. The ensuing slaughter also included the oblate missionaries at their nearby house and chapel, though two of the non-Native wives of officials were spared. Throughout much of the carnage, Big Bear shouted repeatedly at the riflemen to stop, but they refused to listen. By the time the shooting ended, nine men lay dead. A few non-Natives had escaped or been hidden from harm by friends, and Theresa Gowanlock and Theresa Delaney, now widows, found themselves prisoners. Big Bear knew that as well as the missionaries and white men, there was another fatal casualty — his strategy of using peaceful means to obtain improvements in the treatment of Plains peoples.

The chief understood well that people such as Indian Commissioner Dewdney would not know — or would choose to ignore if they knew — that he was not responsible in any way for the violence at Frog Lake on 2 April. Mrs. Gowanlock recalled that the day after the carnage, ". . . Big Bear came into our tent and sitting down beside us told us he was very sorry for what had happened, and cried over it, saying he knew he had so many bad men but had no control over them." The old chief was not ultimately to blame, of course, because his strategy, whether understood or not, had always been a peaceful one. And he was not directly and immediately responsible on the morning of 2 April 1885 because his chieftainship was in abeyance. Because the community saw the situation following reports of the clash at Duck Lake as an emergency, the war chief Wandering Spirit was in control. This meant that the armed men followed his urgings to kill the prisoners rather than listening to Big Bear's repeated pleas to stop the violence. True, the warriors had earlier heeded his request to stop looting the Bay stores, but this restraint probably owed more to their respect for the trading company than to obedience to their civil chief. The complexity and subtlety of Cree political structures always seemed to be a mystery to government officials. Even agent Quinn, who was married to a Native woman and spoke one of the Siouan languages, had not realized that Big Bear was not in charge when he asked the old man's permission to stay in the settlement rather than obey Wandering Spirit's orders to go to the Indian encampment. If the man they called "the Sioux-speaker" had not understood Big Bear's lack of control and responsibility, it was much less likely that other Department of Indian Affairs men, who had long regarded Big Bear with suspicion, would refrain from blaming him for the deaths.

And there was much blame to assign in the Saskatchewan country in the spring of 1885. The encounter at Duck Lake had occurred a week after Riel seized control of the region and declared himself the head of a provisional government on 19 March. This move was an attempt to duplicate the tactics that had worked so well at Red River in 1869–70, but this was not Red River, and the Dominion of Canada did not respond this time with negotiations and concessions. Instead, it used the nearly complete Canadian Pacific Railway to get militiamen to the prairie west, where they teamed up with police and local scouts to mount an attack on the Métis and their headquarters at Batoche. The Métis riflemen, under the leadership of the old buffalo hunter Gabriel Dumont, fought an inconclusive battle with the Canadian forces at Fish Creek, but eventually they were overwhelmed by superior numbers and firepower at Batoche on 12 May. Dumont escaped to the United States, but Riel surrendered to the troops.

The other centre of trouble was the Battleford area, with its heavy concentration of Cree and Assiniboine along the Battle and North Saskatchewan Rivers. There were isolated clashes between armed Indians and officials, in one of which an unpopular official who had offended warriors a few days earlier was shot to death. On the whole, however, the Battleford region remained relatively peaceful, as the Anglican missionary Thomas Clarke noticed when he was out visiting reserves in the days after the Duck Lake clash. However, as Edgar Dewdney had noted in 1879, the Battleford folk were inclined to "unnecessary nervousness," and the local newspaper, the *Saskatchewan Herald*, had been sowing alarm and hostility toward Big Bear and other leaders throughout the early 1880s. The result of trouble elsewhere and exaggerated anxiety at Battleford was the withdrawal of the local populace inside the mounted police post, in what the locals took to calling the siege of Battleford. In reality, there was no such siege, though members of some bands did help themselves to food and other goods from some of the abandoned settlers' houses. In the minds of Battleford's citizens, the complex but relatively benign behaviour of the local reserve communities was translated into a military operation somehow linked to the insurrection led by Riel and Dumont.

Battleford became the centre of important military events later in the spring when Lieutenant-Colonel William Otter arrived to "relieve" the town. Not content to "save" the good citizens of Battleford and vicinity, he set off toward the nearby reserves in pursuit — as he saw it — of the rebels. His force caught up to the retreating bands, who had moved to Cut Knife Hill to get away from the trouble, and suffered a thorough thrashing when they attacked the Cree warriors, who were deployed in a defensive posture under the direction of war chief Fine Day. Eventually, the excitement in the Battleford area died down, too, but the troubles there strengthened the spectre of a general Native uprising in the minds of some officials. Other minor incidents of looting — in the Peace Hills and other areas — were further confirmation for those officials who wanted to find a concerted Native resistance, no doubt involving if not actually led by Big Bear, that had to be crushed, and crushed permanently.

Big Bear's followers strengthened the case against their leader in the days after the massacre of civilians at Frog Lake by laying siege to Fort Pitt. After nearly two weeks of feasting on cattle and enjoying the spoils of Frog Lake, Wandering Spirit and his followers decided that they must take Fort Pitt because it was a strategic threat. Although it had been established as a Hudson's Bay Company post on the north shore of the North Saskatchewan River and still functioned in that capacity, it was also the site of a North West Mounted Police post. It was the red-coated policemen rather than the traders whom Wandering Spirit considered the enemy. Big Bear accompanied the party of over two hundred that made its way to Fort Pitt on 14 April, apparently in the belief that it was still his duty to try to prevent or minimize bloodshed. As matters turned out, there was only one casualty, a policeman who was shot when his return from a scouting assignment unexpectedly brought him into the midst of a parley between Wandering Spirit and the Bay postmaster. The war party finally decided that the police would be allowed to leave peacefully, but the Bay people and others who lived near the fort were to become prisoners. Inspector Francis Dickens was persuaded to leave the fort with his detachment and pass down the river on a scow, while forty-four prisoners joined the Cree camp. Although the taking of Fort Pitt was conducted with miraculously little bloodshed, the destruction of the post and taking of

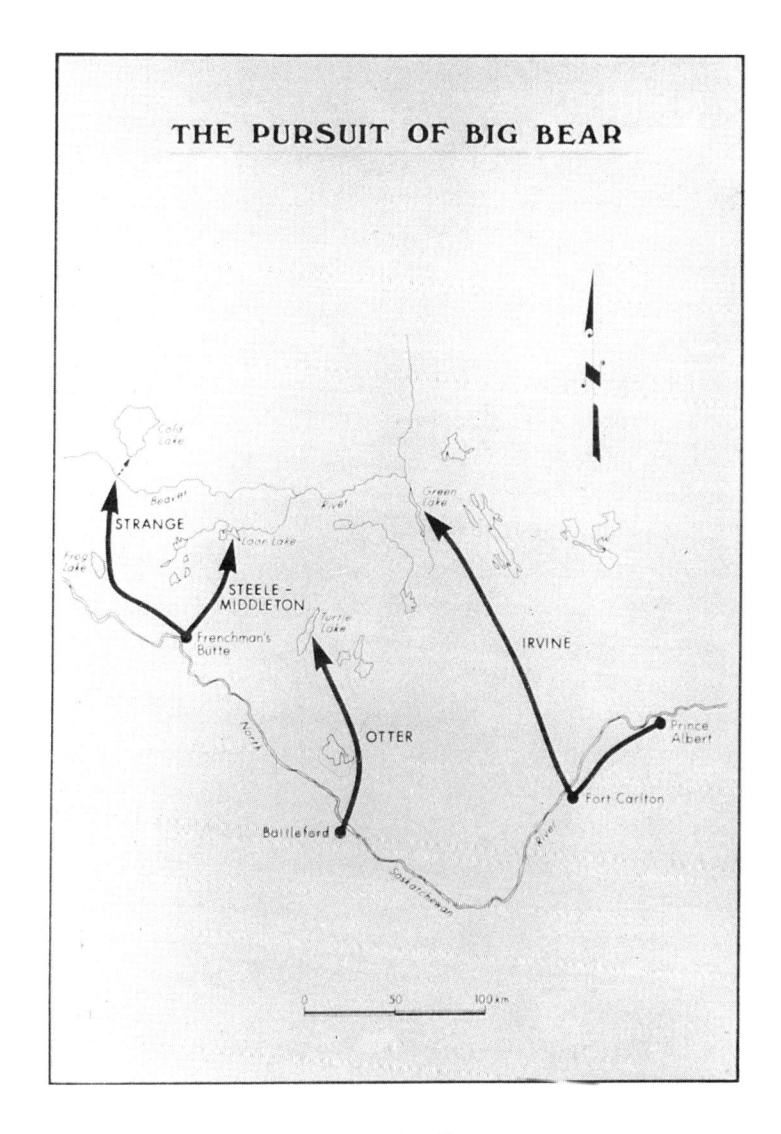

FIGURE 16

Pursuit of Big Bear, 1885.

hostages merely added to the list of Cree offences in the eyes of government officials.

Wandering Spirit and his followers spent another couple of weeks back at Frog Lake enjoying the fruits of their success at Fort Pitt and planning for further action. During this time, Big Bear remained silent, believing that Canada would not fail to respond to the challenges from Riel and the Cree, but he was not in a position to challenge the control of the war chief. Wandering Spirit sent out runners, calling on other Cree along the North Saskatchewan and in the woodlands to rise up, but there was no concerted response to his calls. Some Woods Cree groups joined his camp. Excitement was aroused when a letter, supposedly from Poundmaker, arrived urging Wandering Spirit to join the others in an assault on Battleford. A fact-finding trip by Imasees soon revealed that Poundmaker was under attack by Otter's force. Slowly, Wandering Spirit and his supporters began to realize that the government was not going to be easily or quickly defeated, and Big Bear started to voice his opposition to the continuation of military operations by his followers.

If the martial spirits in the camp were beginning to have second thoughts about their course of action, their doubts were deepened by events in mid-May near Frenchman's Butte, a rise south of the Little Red River that overlooked a valley and wide plateau. Wandering Spirit had taken his large camp there because it was in the Fort Pitt area and a logical jumping-off point for moving farther east or north. A party of almost two hundred militiamen and field artillery under General T.B. Strange caught up to the Cree while they were conducting a Thirst Dance at the base of Frenchman's Butte, and a battle occurred a bit farther north on 28 May. The Cree enjoyed an advantage in occupying rifle pits on elevated land, while the troops had to contend with low, swampy land in the Little Red River ravine, across which they faced the dug-in enemy. On the other hand, the Canadian forces had a nine-pounder artillery piece that did considerable damage when its shells landed in a trench, and inflicted serious psychological harm even when shells fell harmlessly away from

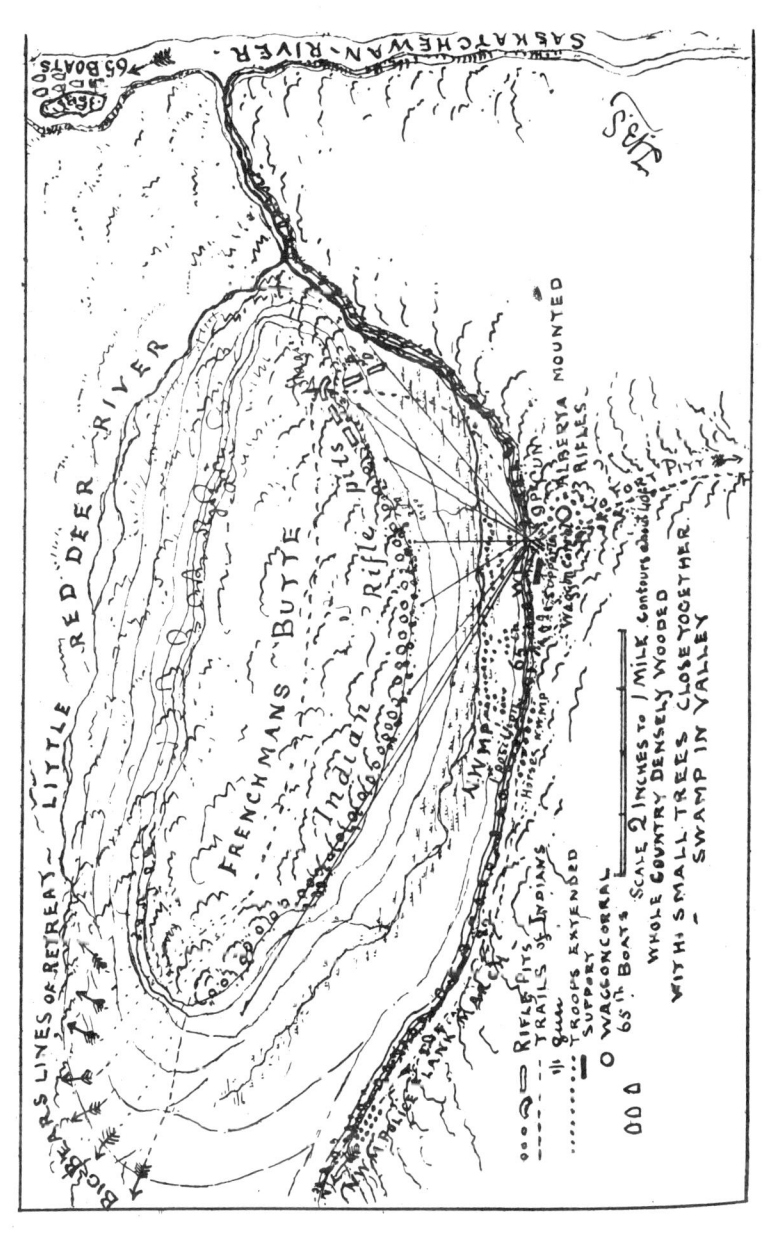

FIGURE 17

General Strange's sketch of Frenchman's Butte.

the Cree warriors. After a few hours of long-distance combat, both sides withdrew. Both Strange and Wandering Spirit had three or four men wounded, and one of the Cree warriors was killed by a nine-pound shell.

Wandering Spirit led his followers and most of the prisoners north into the dense forest, where the war chief hoped Strange's more heavily laden forces could not easily follow. A number of prisoners escaped in the confusion that prevailed at the end of the engagement, but Wandering Spirit was careful to see that the remainder were not harmed and were as well looked after as anyone else in the camp. While on the move, more prisoners, including Theresa Gowanlock and Theresa Delaney, managed to slip away. Some five days after the inconclusive clash near Frenchman's Butte, a group of Sam Steele's scouts, an advance party of a large force directed by Sir Frederick Middleton and Strange, caught up to the Natives in the Loon Lake area. At a narrowing of the lake, which would become known as Steele Narrows, there was another brief encounter, in which Wandering Spirit's forces suffered four fatalities and a number of wounded.

In the aftermath of Steele Narrows, the Cree forces began to break up. As the camp continued moving north to get away from the advancing government forces, a large group of Woods Cree split off and headed west, apparently intending to surrender. Wandering Spirit joined them perhaps because he now thought his honourable course of action was to give himself up, too. The remaining Natives, the Plains Cree who had followed Big Bear, began to make their way slowly and with great difficulty in the general direction of the heart of the Métis resistance, Batoche. By 25 June, this group was facing a crisis: their supplies were exhausted, and they were being pursued by a large force. Several of the minor leaders, including Imasees, chose to head south in the hope of making it over the medicine line to refuge from Canadian retribution. Big Bear decided to take those who remained with him to Fort Carlton, one of his oldest and most familiar places for doing business with the white men. On 4 July, alone except for his youngest son, Horse Child, and a few followers,

FIGURE 18

Big Bear's surrender.

FIGURE 19

Big Bear captured by Strange.

Big Bear was detected on the North Saskatchewan when he asked a Hudson's Bay Company man for some food. When policemen from the Carlton detachment arrived, they found Big Bear, Horse Child, and another man and took them prisoner.

Big Bear now became a pawn in a cruel game that Edgar Dewdney and the government played to defeat once and for all their old rivals, the chiefs who had provided so much peaceful opposition to their policies. Acknowledged leaders of rebel forces, such as Wandering Spirit and Riel, were tried and executed for their roles in the insurrection. So, too, were a number of individuals who had been responsible for individual acts of violence, such as the murder of officials on the reserves south of Battleford. These actions were to be expected, given everything that had happened since Métis and police had clashed at Duck Lake on 26 March. Much more dubious was the action that Canada took against chiefs such as Big Bear and Poundmaker, who had not been responsible for any hostile actions. In Poundmaker's case, it was arguable that his people had not even taken up arms against the government. All they had done was loot abandoned buildings in Battleford and defend themselves from attack at Cut Knife Hill. But such niceties of detail did not deter Dewdney and the government, who were now determined, as John Tobias has explained in "Canada's Subjugation of the Plains Cree, 1879–1885," to impose control through the courts. One way or another, they were going to put the rope around the necks of Big Bear and Poundmaker.

Sixty-year-old Big Bear was helpless in the hands of Canadian law. He and Horse Child were taken to Prince Albert and then to Regina, the territorial capital, where the chief awaited trial. On 11 September, he appeared before a judge and jury of six on four counts of treason-felony, which did not carry the death sentence. Big Bear pleaded not guilty to the charges, and his lawyer called a number of witnesses to show that he had not been in control of his band at Frog Lake, Fort Pitt, Frenchman's Butte, or Loon Lake. Six of the seven prisoners who testified at the trial gave evidence that supported Big Bear's case. Their

FIGURE 20

Horse Child, Big Bear's youngest son, 1885.

FIGURE 21

W.B. Cameron, pro-Big Bear witness, and Horse Child, 1885.

testimony clearly illustrated that Wandering Spirit had been in control, and that Imasees and others of Big Bear's sons had paid no attention to their father. The wife of a Hudson's Bay Company trader testified that Big Bear had warned her family that there might be trouble at Frog Lake, and another Bay man, William Bleasdell Cameron, told the court how Big Bear had finally persuaded a number of young men to stop looting the post there. The prisoner who spoke against Big Bear had to admit on cross-examination that he did not understand Cree, even though he had told the court what Big Bear had said at one point at Frenchman's Butte, and on another point this witness contradicted himself. Throughout all the direct testimony, cross-examination, and lawyers' summation, the elderly chief sat in dignified silence, but also in considerable mystification apparently about the point of the proceedings. The result of the trial had never been in doubt: in a matter of minutes, the jury found Big Bear guilty of treason-felony, but it recommended mercy.

Big Bear's remarks to the court prior to sentencing revealed, as usual, the inner man. For example, the chief could not resist making a joke about his appearance, as he had always tended to do. According to François Dufresne, who acted as an interpreter, Big Bear devoted most of his remarks to a plea on behalf of his people:

> Your Lordship, I am Big Bear, Chief of the Crees. The North West was mine. It belonged to me and to my tribe. For many, many moons I ruled it well. It was when I was away last winter that the trouble started. The young men and the trouble-makers were beyond my control when I returned. They would not listen to my council [sic].
>
> I am old; my face is ugly; my heart is on the ground. In future this land will be ruled by white men with handsome faces. In future moons, if an invader comes to this land, men of my tribe will fight beside the white men. My people then will be of great service to the Great White Mother beyond the big water.

FIGURE 22

Horse Child, Big Bear, and Poundmaker with police and priests, 1885.

When white men were few in this land, I gave them my hand in friendship. No man can ever be witness to any act of violence by Big Bear to any white man. Never did I take the white man's horse. Never did I order any one of my people to one act of violence against the white man. . . .

I ask for pardon and help for my tribe. They are hiding in the hills and trees now afraid to come to white man's government. When the cold moon comes the old and feeble ones, who have done no wrong, will perish. Game is scarce. Can not the men who speak for the White Mother send a pardon to my tribe and send them help?

Because I am Big Bear, Chief of the Crees. Because I have always been a friend of the white man. Because I have always tried to do good for my tribe. I plead with you now; send help and pardon to my people.

The magistrate responded to Mistahimusqua's plea by sentencing the old man to three years at Stony Mountain Penitentiary in Manitoba. Still in chains, the old chief shuffled from the courtroom to begin the final chapter of life under the rope.

PRISONER 103

Stony Mountain was only a worse and longer version of what Big Bear had already suffered. Having failed to keep his people with him on a peaceful course, he had experienced the shame of seeing them led by his son and Wandering Spirit into disaster. Then he had become a prisoner and found out just how humiliating a rope around the neck could be. While in detention in Regina, he and Poundmaker had been persuaded to pose for a photograph with policemen and priests. Big Bear would have hated the fact that Horse Child had been part of the group and thus seen both his father and Poundmaker induced to pose by the gift of pipes. At Stony Mountain, the humiliation continued. Unlike Poundmaker, whose striking build and good looks made

FIGURE 23

On steps of Stony Mountain Penitentiary, 1886.

him an instant favourite, Big Bear was looked down on. The intervention of Poundmaker's adoptive father, Blackfoot chief Crowfoot, spared Poundmaker the indignity of having his hair cut short in conformity with correctional practices. Big Bear received no such consideration. With embarrassingly short hair and wearing a prison uniform, he had to pose with Father Lacombe and Warden Sam Benson on the prison steps to have his picture taken along with Poundmaker, who still had long hair and wore ordinary clothing. Stony Mountain was the depth of Big Bear's winter of humiliation.

Prisoner 103 was subjected to the usual routine and requirements. The irksome periods of being locked up in a cell were relieved only by meals and work. At first, Big Bear was assigned to work in the carpentry shop, but after a few months managed to persuade those in charge to reassign him to caring for the animals in the barn and the warden's private zoo. While some of this work was demeaning, it at least got him out of his cell and into the outdoors more than the other work. And as someone with a close affinity to the spirit of the bear, the chief always enjoyed associating with animals. In such a routine of waking, eating, working, and worrying Big Bear spent the first year of his sentence.

Worry was everpresent for Big Bear. He was anxious about his family, especially young Horse Child. He worried, too, about what had become of his angry son, Imasees, and the more than one hundred people from the band who had accompanied him south toward the medicine line. Imasees, who always referred to himself as Little Bear after 1885, did get to Montana after fleeing the northwest, but he and his people had no end of trouble finding a place where they could settle down. American settler communities and some American-based Indian nations opposed their presence. Over the next few decades, Little Bear and his people would wander around Montana, and even return to Canadian territory. Some settled on a reserve in Alberta and became known as the Montana band, but many others were forced to locate eventually in Montana or remain landless wan-

FIGURE 24

Big Bear and Poundmaker in prison, 1886.

derers in Canada. Big Bear also worried about the fact that by the spring of 1886, some of his fellow Native prisoners were having their sentences commuted and gaining release, while he was stuck looking after the animals. Minor offenders, some with prison sentences longer than Big Bear's, could be released, but Ottawa kept formerly powerful leaders such as Mistahimusqua behind bars. How else to guarantee the continuing subjugation of the Plains Cree?

The old chief's final worry became the government's, too, after Big Bear became seriously ill during the summer of 1886. Obviously, age, a hard life, and now prison conditions were taking their toll, and by autumn officials were anxious that he might die in custody. When the old man began experiencing fainting spells in January 1887, Ottawa realized that it had to act. According to records of the Department of Indian Affairs, Mistawasis and Ahtahkakoop petitioned for his release on the grounds that other chiefs had been freed and that Big Bear's freedom "would be very gratifying to the Cree nation." This was a fitting irony in his humiliation: Mistawasis and Ahtahkakoop had been foremost among the chiefs who had differed with Big Bear by arguing in favour of entering treaty. They, and others such as Poundmaker and Beardy, had tried to accommodate the new power by taking reserves and struggling to learn agriculture, but they had also suffered horribly after the bison economy collapsed. They had thus complained loudly about failure to honour the treaties in the early 1880s, and they had been at the famous council of chiefs at Duck Lake in 1884.

Even though Mistawasis and Ahtahkakoop had not participated in the Métis rebellion in 1885, they and their people also felt the government rope around their necks. For example, Dewdney's emergency measure requiring every reserve resident to obtain a pass from the agent before leaving the reserve had apparently become a permanent policy. The pass system, based neither on statute nor order in council (it was, in fact, a violation of the treaties), would last for decades. Now in spite — perhaps because — of this and other ropes, Mistawasis and Ahtahkakoop

FIGURE 25

Big Bear in prison, 1886.

loaned their names to one final good cause. Supposedly in response to their petition, but in reality to avoid the embarrassment of having the old chief die on its hands, the government released Big Bear in February 1887.

Big Bear spent his last year, from late winter 1887 until mid-January 1888, among old friends on the Little Pine reserve, where one of his daughters, Earth Woman, resided. She looked after her father as he lived out his last months, often alone and bedridden. (Poundmaker had also been released early from prison, and he would soon die while visiting Blackfoot country.) It was fitting in a way that Big Bear ended up on Little Pine. The Little Pine and Poundmaker reserves, which shared a boundary, were a small-scale version of the united Indian territory that Big Bear, Piapot, and other chiefs had tried to fashion in the Cypress Hills and then in the Battleford district by getting reserves in a bloc. That, like so much else of his strategy, had been frustrated, and now he was back to die on Little Pine. The days of glory when he was the civil head of a community of two thousand people were long gone. Now he often lay in bed in a lonely cabin, too ill to go out to see others and ignored by most. During a violent winter storm, he breathed his last on 17 January 1888. He was buried not far from where he died.

"THE NORTH WEST WAS MINE"

Big Bear's legacy would endure. As he had said at the trial, "The North West was mine. It belonged to me and to my tribe. For many, many moons I ruled it well." Although his political strategy of a united and peaceful resistance did not succeed in his lifetime, it served as a model for many Aboriginal people during the long darkness of their subordination to government rule and coerced assimilation between the 1880s and 1950s. Gradually, as Indian pride and assertiveness revived and took political forms in the 1960s and 1970s, it would often be from the ranks of Plains peoples such as Big Bear's Cree that leadership and policy emerged. A century after Mistahimusqua died, the goal that he had pursued so steadfastly if unsuccessfully — to avoid the rope around the neck — once more seemed within reach. And his farsighted, peaceful, and determined pursuit of a fixed goal has inspired many Native leaders from Plains communities in the 1990s.

CHRONOLOGY

1825	Mistahimusqua (Big Bear) is born to Black Powder and an unnamed woman, near Jackfish Lake (in present-day west-central Saskatchewan).
1834	The Hudson's Bay Company establishes Fort Pitt on the North Saskatchewan River.
1838	Big Bear's face is permanently disfigured by a smallpox epidemic that ravages the Indian peoples of the western interior.
1847	While preparing for a raid against the Blackfoot, Big Bear and Black Powder are attacked by an enemy raiding party in the Fort Pitt region. Both escape without harm.
late 1840s	Big Bear marries Sayos, an Ojibwa (Saulteaux) woman with whom he will have two sons and two daughters. Sayos is the first of Big Bear's five wives.
c. 1850–70	Era of the "buffalo wars," in which Plains Cree and Blackfoot are frequently involved in fighting over food resources.
1851	A second son, Imasees (Bad Child), also known as Little Bear (Apistakoos in Cree), is born.
1863	Big Bear again avoids death by staying in Fort Pitt during a Blackfoot attack.
1864–65	Renewed epidemics cause many deaths among Plains peoples.
1865	Black Powder dies; Big Bear becomes chief. He attaches himself to a senior chief, Sweet Grass.
1867	Confederation of the British North American colonies to form the Dominion of Canada occurs on 1 July.
1869–70	Canada obtains the rights to Rupert's Land from the

1870	Hudson's Bay Company, provoking the Red River Resistance by the Métis under Louis Riel. Another smallpox epidemic kills large numbers of Plains peoples.
1871	Sweet Grass and some other chiefs send a message to the Canadian government that they wish to make treaty. Big Bear is not a signatory. The Plains Cree make peace with the Blackfoot, marking the end of the "buffalo wars."
1871–77	Seven numbered treaties are concluded by Canada with various Indian nations in the region stretching from Lake of the Woods to the Rocky Mountains.
1873	The North West Mounted Police are formed; they come west in 1874.
1876	Treaty Six is negotiated at Fort Carlton (in August) and Fort Pitt (in September). Big Bear declines to sign, but promises to return to Fort Pitt in 1877 to meet with the treaty commissioner.
1877	Canada fails to keep its commitment when a minor official, rather than the treaty commissioner, meets Big Bear at Fort Pitt. Big Bear refuses to enter treaty.
1878	Big Bear decides to observe Canada's behaviour for four years, at the end of which he will enter treaty if Canada keeps the treaty terms.
1879	The final collapse of the buffalo economy on the western plains occurs.
1879–82	Big Bear and many other leaders futilely search for the herds, which have nearly been eliminated by overhunting. Several of these forays take Big Bear's following across the medicine line, where they encounter opposition from the American military. In 1879, Big Bear meets Louis Riel in Montana.
1882	Big Bear returns permanently to Canadian territory to avoid the American army. He settles down in the Cypress Hills, where he finally enters treaty in December as a result of increasing starvation among his band.

1883	Big Bear and other chiefs are effectively driven out of the Cypress Hills when the government closes Fort Walsh. He meets with Poundmaker and other chiefs in the Battleford area. The government reduces spending in the Department of Indian Affairs as part of a general retrenchment.
1883–84	Big Bear winters near Fort Pitt and plans his diplomatic strategy of uniting Plains nations.
1884	Big Bear's oldest son, Twin Wolverine, leaves the band as a result of opposition to his father's strategy. A Thirst Dance on the Poundmaker reserve leads to a confrontation with the mounted police. Big Bear attends the council of chiefs at Duck Lake and meets Métis leader Louis Riel. Big Bear unites the northern Cree behind his leadership.
1884–85	The Indian Act is amended, and more police are planned for the northwest to counter the growing restiveness of Plains peoples and Métis.
1885	The clash between police and Métis at Duck Lake on 26 March marks the start of the Northwest Rebellion. On 2 April, nine Euro-Canadians are killed by war chief Wandering Spirit and other warriors of Big Bear's band. Later, Fort Pitt is taken, and brushes with troops occur at Frenchman's Butte and Loon Lake. Big Bear surrenders in July; he is tried, convicted, and sentenced to three years' imprisonment. Imasees (Little Bear) escapes to Montana.
1886	Big Bear becomes seriously ill while in Stony Mountain Penitentiary in Manitoba.
1887	The government releases him after receiving a petition from "loyal chiefs" in the Fort Carlton area. He goes to live with his daughter on Little Pine reserve in the Battleford area.
1888	Big Bear dies on Little Pine reserve on 17 January and is buried nearby.

WORKS CONSULTED

Allen, Robert S. "Big Bear." *Saskatchewan History* 25.1 (1972): 1–17.
——— . "The Breaking of Big Bear." *Horizon Canada* 5 (1986): 1190–95.
Beal, Bob, and Rod Macleod. *Prairie Fire: The 1885 North-West Rebellion.* Edmonton: Hurtig, 1984.
"Big Bear Rises to Explain." *Saskatchewan Herald* [Battleford, SK Territory] 5 Aug. 1882: 2.
Cameron, William Bleasdell. *The War Trail of Big Bear.* Toronto: Ryerson, [1927].
Canada. Department of Indian Affairs. *Annual Report of the Department of Indian Affairs.* . . . 1880–87.
——— . ——— . Records, RG 10. Microfilm. National Archives of Canada, Ottawa.
Clarke (Thomas) Papers. Saskatchewan Archives Board, Saskatoon.
Davin, Nicholas F. "Report on Industrial Schools for Indians and Half-Breeds." 14 Mar. 1879. Macdonald Papers.
Dempsey, Hugh A. *Big Bear: The End of Freedom.* Vancouver: Douglas, 1984.
——— . *Crowfoot, Chief of the Blackfeet.* 1972. Edmonton: Hurtig, 1976.
——— . "The Fearsome Fire Wagons." *The CPR West: The Iron Road and the Making of a Nation.* Ed. Dempsey. Vancouver: Douglas, 1984. 54–69.
Dempsey, James. "Little Bear's Band: Canadian or American Indians?" *Alberta History* 41.4 (1993): 2–9.
Dewdney (Edgar) Papers, M 320. Glenbow Archives, Calgary.
Dickason, Olive Patricia. *Canada's First Nations: A History of Founding Peoples from Earliest Times.* Toronto: McClelland, 1992.
Dion, Joseph F. *My Tribe the Crees.* Ed. Hugh A. Dempsey. 1979. Calgary: Glenbow-Alberta Inst., 1993.
Dufresne, François. "Defence of Big Bear." Narr. to Humphrey Gratz. *Western Producer* 16 June 1983: 10–11.
Erasmus, Peter. *Buffalo Days and Nights.* Narr. to Henry Thompson. Calgary: Glenbow-Alberta Inst., 1976.
Fraser, W.B. "Big Bear, Indian Patriot." *Alberta Historical Review* 14.2 (1966): 1–13.

Friesen, Gerald. *The Canadian Prairies: A History.* Toronto: U of Toronto P, 1984.

Friesen, Jean. "Magnificent Gifts: The Treaties of Canada with the Indians of the Northwest 1869–76." *Transactions of the Royal Society of Canada* 5th ser. 1 (1986): 41–51.

Gowanlock, Theresa, and Theresa Delaney. *Two Months in the Camp of Big Bear: The Life and Adventures of Theresa Gowanlock and Theresa Delaney.* Parkdale, ON: Times, 1885 [CIHM 30360].

Hardisty (Richard) Papers, M 477. Glenbow Archives, Calgary.

Jefferson, Robert. *Fifty Years on the Saskatchewan.* Canadian North-West Historical Society Publications 1.5. Battleford, SK: Canadian North-West Historical Soc., 1929.

Lucas (Samuel B.) Papers, M 699. Glenbow Archives, Calgary.

Macdonald (John A.) Papers, MG 26 A. National Archives of Canada, Ottawa.

Macleod, R.C. *The North West Mounted Police 1873–1919.* The Canadian Historical Association Booklets 31. Ottawa: Canadian Historical Assn., 1978.

———. *The NWMP and Law Enforcement 1873–1905.* Toronto: U of Toronto P, 1976.

Mandelbaum, David G. *The Plains Cree: An Ethnographic, Historical, and Comparative Study.* Canadian Plains Studies 9. 1979. Regina: Canadian Plains Research Center, U of Regina, 1987.

McDougall, John. *George Millward McDougall, the Pioneer, Patriot and Missionary.* Toronto: Briggs; Montreal: Coates; Halifax: Huestis, 1888.

McMillan, Alan D. *Native Peoples and Cultures of Canada: An Anthropological Overview.* Vancouver: Douglas, 1988.

Miller, J.R. *Skyscrapers Hide the Heavens: A History of Indian-White Relations in Canada.* Rev. ed. Toronto: U of Toronto P, 1991.

———, ed. *Sweet Promises: A Reader on Indian-White Relations in Canada.* Toronto: U of Toronto P, 1991.

Milloy, John S. *The Plains Cree: Trade, Diplomacy and War, 1790 to 1870.* Manitoba Studies in Native History 4. Winnipeg: U of Manitoba P, 1988.

Morris, Alexander. *The Treaties of Canada with the Indians of Manitoba and the North-West Territories. . . .* 1880. Saskatoon: Fifth House, 1991.

North West Mounted Police Papers, RG 18. National Archives of Canada, Ottawa.

Reed (Hayter) Papers, MG 29 E 106. National Archives of Canada, Ottawa.

Saskatchewan Herald [Battleford, SK Territory] [microfilm] 5 Aug. 1882; 4 Aug. 1883; 8 Mar. 1884.

Stanley, George F.G. "An Account of the Frog Lake Massacre." Narr. to A.E. Peterson. *Alberta Historical Review* 4.1 (1956): 23–27.

———. *The Birth of Western Canada: A History of the Riel Rebellions*. 1936. Toronto: U of Toronto P, 1960.

Tobias, John L. "Canada's Subjugation of the Plains Cree, 1879–1885." *Canadian Historical Review* 64 (1983): 519–48.

———. "Indian Reserves in Western Canada: Indian Homelands or Devices for Assimilation." *Approaches to Native History in Canada: Papers of a Conference Held at the National Museum of Man, October, 1975*. Ed. D.A. Muise. National Museum of Man Mercury Series; History Division Paper 25. Ottawa: National Museum of Man [Canadian Museum of Civilization], 1977. 89–103.

———. "The Origins of the Treaty Rights Movement in Saskatchewan." *1885 and After: Native Society in Transition*. Ed. F. Laurie Barron and James B. Waldram. Proc. of a conference at U of Saskatchewan, Saskatoon, May 1985. Canadian Plains Proceedings 16. Regina: Canadian Plains Research Center, U of R, 1986. 241–52.

Woodcock, George. *Gabriel Dumont: The Métis Chief and His Lost World*. Edmonton: Hurtig, 1975.

imprimerie gagné ltée

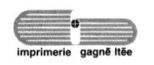

PRINTED IN CANADA